The
Practical Stylist

The
Practical Stylist

SECOND EDITION

Sheridan Baker

UNIVERSITY OF MICHIGAN

Thomas Y. Crowell Company

NEW YORK   ESTABLISHED 1834

L. C. Card 69-19298
ISBN: 0-690-64998-3

Manufactured in the United States of America
by Vail-Ballou Press, Inc., Binghamton, N.Y.

First Printing, March, 1969
Second Printing, June, 1969
Third Printing, October, 1969
Fourth Printing, June, 1970
Fifth Printing, August, 1970

To Sally

Preface

THIS IS A RHETORIC primarily for freshman English, but it has also proved useful to the advanced student and to many others who have found themselves facing a blank page and the problems of exposition. From the freshman's first essay through the senior's last paper (and on through the doctoral dissertation and the company's annual report), the expository problems are always the same. Indeed, they all come down to two fundamental questions: one of form, one of style. And even form is a spatial styling. Since, in general, writing well is writing in style, I have found it practical to teach writing almost as a tactile art, in which the student learns how to shape his material and bring out the grain to best advantage. Hence *The Practical Stylist*—now revised extensively.

I have added a number of exercises throughout, and two new chapters, on "Writing Good Sentences" and on "Correcting Bad Sentences," bringing together remarks on awkward writing that had earlier appeared in the chapters on "Sentences" and "Words." I have also added a short chapter on "Grammar" and a short section on using the library. I have brought the section on usage up to date, expanding it and moving it to the back of the book as "A Glossary of Usage." But, in its contents, its size, and its practical intent, the book remains essentially the same.

I mean the book also to be practical in its brevity. Most handbooks on writing seem too big, too wordy, too involved. They seem to get mired in their own diligence and to stay stuck on the student's shelf. This book aims to travel light, to cover the ground without inordinate deliberation. I have included only what seems useful and essential. I think teachers will miss nothing that a more voluminous handbook might contain.

To be sure, I omit some of the pedagogical favorites, such as definition and syllogistic reasoning, because I believe them secondary to more basic processes, which in fact manage most of the refinements without worrying about them. I emphasize argument, because I believe that argument subsumes all other expository principles, and that it teaches clearly and easily the firmest organization. So I begin with the argumentative thesis and include only a few exercises in simple exposition.

Many handbooks begin with simple units and build upward. I have found the opposite approach far more efficient. Once the student can push his material into a single argumentative thesis and can grasp the large essentials of structural arrangement, he can proceed easily to the smaller and smaller elements, which get the more powerful as they decrease in size—to paragraphs, to sentences and their punctuation, and on to the heart of the matter, to words, where the real dynamite, the real color and music, is.

I have included exercises—in thesis-making, in paragraphing, in writing various kinds of sentences and punctuating them, in using words and spelling them, in handling various figures of speech. I have tried to encourage the student to play with language, to write unusual and complicated sentences for exercise, to juggle with words, much as the new courses in elementary mathematics start with numerical games and puzzles.

At this point the student should be ready for "Three Excursions," a chapter intended to sharpen his sense of language by exercises in how to put his personal experience directly into words, in how *not* to write, and in how to write irony. Then follows a chapter on the research paper, bringing the student's expository skills fully to bear. The book concludes with an appendix on usage, including some practical prescriptions for good writing. Inside the front cover is a list against which the student may check his work; inside the back cover, a set of symbols for marking errors. The book serves well alone—if the teacher likes to concentrate on his students' writing, in weekly essays arising from the exercises—or in company with an anthology of readings.

The teacher will find plenty of room for his own course. He will undoubtedly find opportunity for that almost necessary bonus of academic gratification, disagreeing with the book—out of which much of our best teaching comes. He will certainly find a great deal that is familiar. Nothing here is really new. I am simply describing the natural linguistic facts discovered again and again by the heirs of Aristotle, in which lineage I seem inescapably to belong. For I have found that the one practical need in all writing is to mediate gracefully between opposite possibilities, between simplicity and complexity, clarity and shade, economy and plenitude, the particular and the general. I hope this book will help student and teacher to shoot the wickets pleasantly and well.

S. B.

Ann Arbor, Michigan
January, 1969

Acknowledgments

I WISH TO ACKNOWLEDGE my great debt to the teachers who, from the testing of some fifteen thousand classrooms, have given me their encouragement and their suggestions. I wish especially to thank Mrs. Fran Measley of Santa Barbara, California, for inventing "The Keyhole" (p. 25), and Mr. John Antico of Lansing Community College (Michigan) for thoughtful comments. I am no less grateful to the many individual students and private citizens who have written me from as far away as Kenya and as near home as Ann Arbor.

I am delighted to be able to name again those persons who influenced, in one way or another, the first edition of *The Practical Stylist:* Mark Schorer, Ullman Kilgore, Mrs. Campbell Bonner. I am glad to cite again those writers from whose work I first adapted one idea or another: Robert C. Waddell, Paul Roberts, Rudolf Flesch. Again I am happy to record my deep gratitude to my first editor, Novello Grano, without whose rigorous eye this book would have been much the poorer, and without whose initial suggestion it would probably not have been written at all.

Contents

The
Practical Stylist

1. Thesis

THE STYLISTIC APPROACH

STYLE IN WRITING is something like style in a car, a woman, or a Greek temple—a kind of linear mastery of materials that stands out from the landscape and compels a second look. It is some unique and unobtrusive synthesis of matter available to everyone; and, if a writer's style is really good, it will hang in the reader's memory and continue to bring wonder to the mind. Style is the product of a craftsman alive to experience and to the possibilities and the obstinacies in the material he works. It is a labor of love, and like love it can bring pleasure and satisfaction. A writer should like words the way some people like stones. He should like phrasing and syntax, and the very punctuation that keeps them straight. His interest in language should equal his interest in what he has to say, or he will never get the two together in any way he can call his own. He will never convince or delight, or get a second look.

This is not to say that style is only for the gifted. Quite the contrary. There *is* a certain mystery about writing, just as there is about life. But the stylistic side of writing is, in fact, the only side that can be analyzed and learned. The stylistic approach is the practical approach: you learn some things to do and not to do, as you would learn strokes in tennis. Your ultimate game is up to you, but you can at least begin in good form. Naturally, it takes practice. You have to keep at it. Like the doctor and the lawyer and the golfer and the tennis player, you just keep practicing—even to write a practically perfect letter. But if you like the game, you can probably learn to play it well. You will at least be able to write a respectable sentence, and to express your thoughts clearly, without excessive puffing and flailing.

In the essay, as in business, trying to get started and getting off on the wrong foot account for most of our lost motion. So you will start by learning how to find a thesis, which will virtually organize your essay for you. Next you will study the relatively simple structure of the essay, and the structure of the paragraph—the architecture of spatial styling. Then, for exercise, you will experiment with various styles of sentence, playing with length and complexity. And finally you will get down to words themselves. Here is where writing tells; and here, as in ancient times, you will be in touch with the mystery. But again, there are things to do and things not to do, and these can be learned. So, to begin.

WHERE ESSAYS FAIL

You can usually blame a bad essay on a bad beginning. If your essay falls apart, it probably has no primary idea to hold it together. "What's the big idea?" we used to ask. The phrase will serve as a reminder that you must find the "big idea" behind your several smaller thoughts and musings before you start to write. In the beginning was the *logos,* says the Bible—the idea, the plan, caught in a flash as if in a single word. Find your *logos,* and you are ready to round out your essay and set it spinning.

The central idea, or thesis, is your essay's life and spirit. If your thesis is sufficiently clear, it will organize your material almost automatically and so obviate elaborate planning. If you do not find a thesis, your essay will be a tour through the miscellaneous. An essay replete with scaffolds and catwalks—"We have just seen this; now let us turn to this"—is an essay in which the inhering idea is weak or nonexistent. A purely expository and descriptive essay, one simply about "Cats," for instance, will have to rely on outer scaffolding alone (some orderly progression from Persia to Siam) since it really has no idea at all. It is all subject, all cats, instead of an embodied idea *about* cats.

THE ARGUMENTATIVE EDGE

Find your thesis. The *about*-ness puts an argumentative edge on the subject. When you have something to say *about* cats, you have found your underlying idea. You have something to defend, something to fight about: not just "Cats," but "The cat is really man's best friend." Now the hackles on all dog men are rising, and you have an argument on your hands. You have something to prove; you have a thesis.

"What's the big idea, Mac?" Let the impudence in that time-honored demand remind you that the best thesis is a kind of affront to somebody, a fly in the facial ointment of all conventions. No one will be very much interested in listening to you deplete the thesis "The dog is man's best friend." Everyone knows that already. Even the dog-lovers will be uninterested, convinced that they know better than you. But the cat . . . .

So it is with any unpopular idea. The more unpopular the viewpoint and the stronger the push against convention, the stronger the thesis and the more energetic the essay. Compare the energy in "Democracy is good" with that in "Communism is good," for instance. The first is filled with platitudes, the second with plutonium. By the same token, if you can find the real energy in "Democracy is good," if you can get down through the sand to where the roots and water are, you will have a real essay, for the opposition against which you generate your energy is the heaviest in the world: boredom. Probably the most energetic thesis of all, the greatest inner organizer, is some tired old truth that you cause to jet with new life, making the old ground green again.

To find a thesis is to narrow and define your subject to a workable size. Under "Cats" you must deal with all felinity from the jungle up, carefully partitioning the eons and areas, the tigers and tabbies, the sizes and shapes. The minute you proclaim the cat the friend of man, you have pared away whole categories and chapters and need only think up the arguments sufficient to overwhelm the opposition, or at least to leave them scratching their ears and panting. So, put an argumentative edge on your subject —and you will have found your thesis.

Simple exposition, to be sure, has its uses. You may want to tell someone how to build a dog house, how to can asparagus, how to follow the outlines of relativity, or even how to write an essay. Performing a few exercises in simple exposition will no doubt sharpen your insight into the problems of finding orderly sequences, of considering how best to lead your readers through the hoops, of writing clearly and accurately. It will also illustrate how much finer and surer an argument is.

You will see that picking an argument immediately simplifies the problems so troublesome in straight exposition: the defining, the partitioning, the narrowing of the subject. Actually, you can put an argumentative edge on the flattest of expository subjects. "How to build a dog house" might become "Building a dog house is a thorough introduction to the building trades, including architecture and mechanical engineering." "Canning asparagus" might become "An asparagus patch is a course in economics." "Relativity" might become "Relativity is not the inscrutable mystery many suppose." You have simply assumed that you have a loyal Opposition consisting of the uninformed, the uninterested, and the scornful. You have given your subject its edge; you have limited and organized it at a single stroke. Pick an argument, then, and you will automatically be defining and narrowing your subject, and all the partitions you don't need will fold up. Instead of dealing with things, subjects, and pieces of subjects, you will be dealing with an idea and its consequences.

Sharpen your thesis. Come out with your subject pointed. Take a stand, make a judgment of value. Be reasonable, but don't be timid. Think of your thesis, your main idea, as a debating question —"Resolved: Old age pensions must go"—then take out the "Resolved" when you actually write the subject down. But your resolution will be even stronger, your essay clearer and tighter, if you can sharpen your thesis one punctilio further—"Resolved: Old age pensions must go because_____." Fill in that blank and your worries are practically over.

Try, for instance: "Old age pensions must go because they are making people irresponsible." I don't know at all if that is true, and neither will you until you write your way into it, considering probabilities and alternatives and objections, and especially the underlying assumptions. In fact, no one, no master sociologist or future historian, can tell absolutely if it is true, so multiplex are the causes in human affairs, so endless and tangled the consequences. The basic assumption—that irresponsibility is growing —may be entirely false. No one can tell absolutely. But by the same token, your guess may be as good as another's. At any rate, you are now ready to write. You have found your *logos*.

Now you can put your well-pointed thesis on a card on the wall in front of you to keep from drifting off target. But you will now want to dress it for the public, to burnish it and make it comely. Suppose you try:

Old age pensions, perhaps more than anything else, are eroding our heritage of personal and familial responsibility.

But is this true? Perhaps you had better try something like:

Despite their many advantages, old age pensions may actually be eroding our heritage of personal and familial responsibility.

This is really your thesis, and you can write that down on a scrap of paper too.

Believe in your thesis. Notice how your original assertion has mellowed. And not because you have resorted to cheap tactics, though tactics may get a man to the same place, but rather because you have brought it under critical inspection. You have asked yourself what is true in it: what can (and cannot) be assumed true, what can (and cannot) be proved true. And you have asked where you yourself stand.

You should, indeed, look for a thesis you believe in, something you can even get enthusiastic about. Arguing on both sides of a question, as debaters do, is no doubt good exercise. It breaks up old ground and uncovers what you can and do believe, at least for the moment. But the argument without the belief will be hollow. You can hardly persuade anyone if you can't persuade yourself.

Conversely, you must test your belief with all the objections you can think of, just as you have already tested your first proposition about old age pensions. First, you have acknowledged the most evident objection—that the opposition's view must have some merit—by starting your final version with "Despite their many advantages . . . ." Second, you have gone a little deeper by seeing that in your bold previous version you had, with the words *are eroding*, begged the question of whether responsibility is in fact undergoing erosion; that is, you had silently assumed that responsibility *is* being eroded. This is one of the oldest tricks of logic. To "beg the question," by error or intent, is to take for granted that which the opposition has not granted, to assume as already proved that which is yet to be proved. But you have saved yourself. You have changed *are eroding* to *may be eroding*. You have gone further in deleting the *perhaps more than anything else*. You have come closer to the truth.

Truth, for many, is something mystical and awesome; for others, something remote and impractical. And how can you presume to go around stating theses before you have studied your subject from all angles, made several house-to-house surveys, and read everything ever written? A natural uncertainty and feeling of ignorance, and a misunderstanding of what truth is, can well inhibit you from finding a thesis. But no one knows everything. No one would write anything if he waited until he did. To a great extent, as I have already said, the writing of a thing is the learning of it.

So, first, make yourself a desperate thesis and get into the arena. This is probably solution enough. If your thesis becomes increasingly untrue, no matter how hard you push it, turn it around and use the other end. If your convictions have begun to falter with:

> **Despite their many advantages, old age pensions undermine responsibility . . . .**

try it the other way around, with something like:

> **Although old age pensions may offend the rugged individualist, they relieve much want and anxiety, and they dispel much familial resentment.**

You will now have a beautiful command of all the objections to your new position. And you will have learned something about human fallibility and the nature of truth.

We *are* fallible. Furthermore, the truth about our most teasing and insistent questions usually lies somewhere beyond our fingertips. You may know, or guess, the truth; you may believe that such-and-such is so. But often you can never know it or prove it in any physical way. And neither can anyone else. You can only take it on faith—as much faith as your temperament allows.

Differences of opinion, they say, make a horse race, and we often hear that one man's opinion is as good as another's. But the race rather quickly proves that one man's opinion was wrong. But the opinion that Man O' War is the greatest three-year-old of all time is beyond proof. "All time" is a long time. All the returns are not yet in. And much of the past is beyond reach. But even this opinion, though we can never know for certain, is either right or wrong. All we can do is to weigh the probabilities, and believe.

Persuade your reader. Once you believe in your proposition, you will discover that proving it is really a venture in persuasion. You have made a thesis, an hypothesis really—an opinion as to what the truth seems to be from where you stand, with the information you have. Oddly enough, your proof has nothing to do with *making* that opinion right or wrong. If it is right, it is right; if wrong, wrong—with or without proof. Your thesis is not "more right" after you have backed it with proof: it is merely shown to have been right all the time. Whether you got it in a flash or in a year's careful analysis makes no difference. You knew it from the moment of your conviction; now the skeptical reader must believe it too. You must give him enough evidence to persuade him that what you say is probably true, finding arguments that will stand up in the marketplace and survive the public haggle. You must find public reasons for your private convictions.

Don't apologize. "In my opinion," the beginner will write repeatedly, until he seems to be saying "It is only *my* opinion, after all, so it can't be worth much." He has failed to realize that his whole essay represents his opinion—of what the truth of the matter is. Don't make your essay a letter to Diary, or to Mother, or to Teacher, a confidential report of what happened to you last night as you agonized upon a certain question. "*To me*, Robert Frost is a great poet"—this is really writing about yourself. You are only confessing private convictions. To find the "public reasons" often requires no more than a trick of grammar: a shift from "*To me*, Robert Frost is . . ." to "Robert Frost is . . ."; from "*I thought* the book was good" to "The book is good"; from you and your room last night to your subject and what it *is*. The grammatical shift represents a whole change of viewpoint, a shift from self to subject. You become the man of reason, showing the reader around firmly, politely, and persuasively.

Once you have effaced yourself from your thesis, once you have erased *to me* and *in my opinion* and all such signs of amateur terror, you may later let yourself back into the essay for emphasis or graciousness: "Mr. Watson errs, I think, precisely at this point." You can thus ease your most tentative or violent assertions, and show that you are polite and sensible, reasonably sure of your position but aware of the possibility of error. Again: the man of reason. But omitting the *I* altogether is better than writing a junior autobiography of your discoveries and doubts.

Now, with clear conscience, you are ready to write. Your single thesis-sentence has magically conjured up your essay. All you need now is some form to put it in.

1. Convert each of the following general subjects into a debating resolution ("Resolved: Cats make better pets than dogs"; "Resolved: Old age pensions must go"):

tropical fish	teen-agers
the United Nations	foreign languages
knitting	badminton
fraternities	stamps
budgets	history
grammar	shoes
apples	books

2. Pick three from your list of debating resolutions; drop the "Resolved"; and add a "because _____" ("Old age pensions must go because they are making people irresponsible").

3. Now smooth out these three theses for public appearance, omitting the direct statement of *because*, and adding qualifications ("Despite their many advantages, old age pensions may actually be eroding our heritage of personal and familial responsibility").

4. Now turn your three smoothed theses completely around, so that they assert the opposite ("Although old age pensions may offend the rugged individualist, they relieve much want and anxiety, and they dispel much familial resentment").

2. Structure

Beginning, Middle, and End

Build your essay in three parts. There really is no other way.
As Aristotle long ago pointed out, works that spin their way along
through time need a beginning, a middle, and an end to give them
the stability of spatial things like paintings and statues. You need
a clear beginning to give your essay character and direction, so
the reader can tell where he is going and can look forward with
expectation. Your beginning, of course, will set forth your thesis.
You need a middle to amplify and fulfill. This will be the body of
your argument. You need an end to let the reader know that he has
arrived and where. This will be your final paragraph, a summation
and reassertion of your theme.

Give your essay the three-part *feel* of beginning, middle, and
end. The mind likes this triple order. Three has always been a
magic number. The woodcutter always has three sons, or three
daughters; even the physical universe has three dimensions. Three
has a basic psychological appeal as strong as a triangle or pyramid
—especially with words and music, which the mind must pick up
out of the air and assemble for itself into something like a spatial
structure, a total impression. Many a freshman's essay has no structure and leaves no impression. It is all chaotic middle. It has no
beginning, it just begins; it has no end, it just stops, fagged out at
two in the morning.

The beginning must feel like a beginning, not like an accident.
It should be a full paragraph that lets your reader gently into
the subject and culminates with your thesis. The end, likewise,
should be a full paragraph, one that drives the point home, pushes

9

the implications wide, and brings the reader to rest, back on middle C, giving a sense of completion with the tonic. The next chapter describes these two kinds of paragraph more fully. The middle, however, being the bulk of your essay, needs further structural consideration now.

MIDDLE TACTICS

Arrange your points in order of increasing interest. Once your thesis has sounded the challenge, your reader's interest is probably at its highest pitch. He wants to see how you can prove so outrageous a thing, or to see what the arguments are for this thing he has always believed but never tested. Each step of the way into your demonstration, he is learning more of what you have to say. But unfortunately his interest may be relaxing as it becomes satisfied: the reader's normal line of attention is a progressive decline, arching down like a wintry graph. Against this decline you must oppose your forces, so that the vector of your reader's interest will continue at least on the horizontal, with no sag, and preferably with an upward swing:

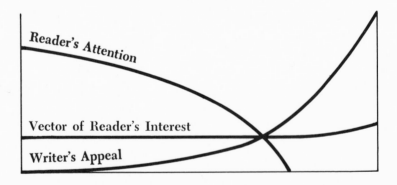

This is the basic principle for organizing the middle of your essay. Save your best till last. It is as simple as that.

Each successive item of your presentation should be more interesting than the last, or you will suddenly seem anticlimactic. Actually, minor regressions of interest make no great difference so long as the whole tendency is uphill and your last item clearly the best. Suppose, for example, you were to undertake the cat thesis.

You decide that four points would make up the case, and that you might arrange them in the following order of increasing interest: (1) cats are affectionate but make few demands; (2) cats actually can look out for themselves; (3) cats have, in fact, proved extremely useful to man throughout history in controlling mice and other plaguy rodents; (4) cats satisfy some basic need in man for a touch of the jungle, savagery in repose, ferocity in silk, and have been worshiped for the exotic power they still seem to represent, even dozing on the banister. You may find, as you write, thinking things up, that Number 1 is developing attractive or amusing instances, and perhaps even virtually usurping the whole essay. Numbers 2, 3, and 4 should then be moved in ahead as interesting but brief preliminaries. Your middle structure, thus, should range from least important to most important, from simple to complex, from narrow to broad, from pleasant to hilarious, from mundane to metaphysical—whatever "leasts" and "mosts" your subject suggests.

Acknowledge and dispose of the opposition. Your cat essay, because it is moderately playful, can proceed rather directly, throwing only an occasional bone of concession to the dogs. But a serious controversial argument demands one organizational consideration beyond the simple structure of ascending interest. Although you have taken your stand firmly as a *pro*, you will have to allow scope to the *con*'s, or you will seem not to have thought much about your subject. The more opposition you can manage as you carry your point, the more triumphant you will seem, like a man on a high wire daring the impossible.

The basic organizing principle here is to get rid of the opposition first, and to end on your own side. Probably you will have already organized your thesis-sentence in a perfect pattern for your *con-pro* argument:

Despite their many advantages, old age pensions . . . .
Although dogs are fine pets, cats . . . .

The subordinate clause states the subordinate part of your argument, which is your concession to the *con* viewpoint; your main clause states your main argument. As the subordinate clause comes first in your thesis-sentence, so with the subordinate argument in your essay. Sentence and essay both reflect a natural psychological principle. You want, and the reader wants, to get the boys off the street so the men can have room. And you want to end on your best foot. (You might try putting the opposition last, just to see how peculiarly the last word insists on seeming best, and how, when stated last by you, the opposition's case seems to be your own.)

If the opposing arguments seem relatively slight and brief, you can get rid of them all together in one paragraph before you get down to your case. Immediately after your beginning, which has stated your thesis, you write a paragraph of concession: "Of course, security is a good thing. No one wants old people begging." And so on to the end of the paragraph, deflating every conceivable objection. Then back to the main line: "But the price in moral decay is too great." The structure might be diagrammed something like this:

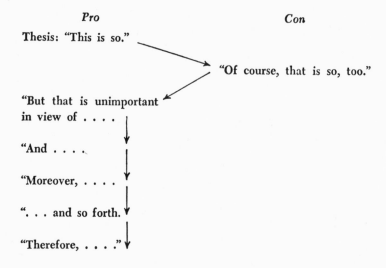

Pro

Thesis: "This is so."

Con

"Of course, that is so, too."

"But that is unimportant in view of . . . .

"And . . . .

"Moreover, ...

". . . and so forth.

"Therefore, ..."

If the opposition is more considerable, demolish it point by point, using a series of *con*'s and *pro*'s. Each paragraph can be a small argument that presents the opposition, then knocks it flat— a kind of Punch and Judy show in series: "We must admit that . . . . But . . . ." And down goes the poor old opposition again. The structural line might look like this:

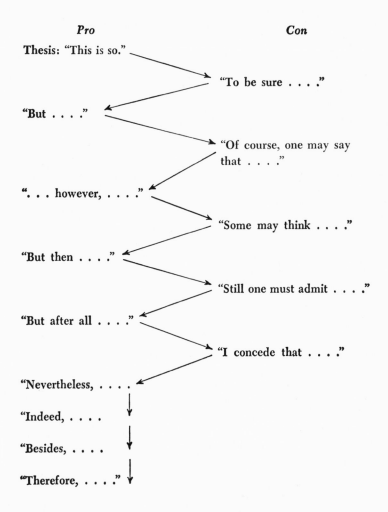

Pro   *Con*

Thesis: "This is so."

"To be sure . . . ."

"But . . . ."

"Of course, one may say that . . . ."

". . . however, ..."

"Some may think . . . ."

"But then . . . ."

"Still one must admit . . . ."

"But after all . . . ."

"I concede that . . . ."

"Nevertheless, ...

"Indeed, ...

"Besides, ...

"Therefore, ..."

You will notice that *but* and *however* are always guides for the *pro*'s, serving as switches back to the main line. You will do well to make yourself two lists of these switching words and phrases, one for the *pro*'s and one for the *con*'s, adding to those I have used above, to get the feel of the argumentative turn and to have them handy. *But, however,* and *Nevertheless* are the basic *pro*'s. *But* always heads its turning sentence (not followed by a comma); *Nevertheless* usually does (followed by a comma). I am sure, however, that *however* is always better buried in the sentence between commas; *But* for the quick turn; the inlaid *however* for the more elegant sweep.

Run your comparisons point by point. Don't write all about sheep for three pages, then all about goats. Every time you say something about a sheep, say something comparable about a goat, pelt for pelt, horn for horn, beard for beard. Otherwise your essay will fall in two, and any sheep-points you want to develop among the goats will have to be repeated. The tendency to organize comparisons by halves is so strong that you will probably find you have fallen into it unawares, and in rewriting you will have to reorganize everything point for point—still arranging your pairs of points from least important to most. Finally, the only comparison worth making is one that aims to demonstrate a superiority, one, that is, with a thesis—"Resolved: Sheep are more useful than goats."

Now you have almost finished your essay. You have found a thesis. You have worked it into a decent beginning. You have then worked out a convincing middle, with your arguments presented in a sequence of ascending interest; you have used up all your points and said your say. You and your argument are both exhausted. But don't stop. You need an end, or the whole thing will unravel in your reader's mind. You need to buttonhole him in a final paragraph, to imply "I told you so" without saying it, to hint at the whole round experience he has just had, and to leave him convinced, satisfied, and admiring. One more paragraph will do it: beginning, middle, *and* end.

EXERCISES

1. Write five *con*-and-*pro* thesis sentences, beginning "Although . . . ."

2. Write a 500-word description of a process you know well—how to plan a vacation, how to play winning croquet, how an internal combustion engine works. This is straight exposition. It will introduce you to the fine dry air of objectivity; to the problem of laying out in orderly sequence, for the reader's gathering comprehension, details that are in fact simultaneous; and to the difficulty of finding the clear, accurate, and descriptive phrase.

3. Now find a thesis that will change this description into an argument making some statement *about* the subject: the best-planned vacations can be disastrous; winning croquet is no child's play; what's under

the hood is really no mystery. Rewrite the first paper using your new thesis and using, in some way, everything you said before.

4. Write a series of three-paragraph argumentative essays, conveying a thorough sense of beginning, middle, and end. (One of the best stylists I know, a German whose command of English is a living rebuke to American education, told me that his grasp of organization comes from having had to write, through a number of grammar-school years, nothing but three-paragraph essays. The treatment appears to have been excellent.)

5. Take a conventional proposition, like "Democracy is good" or "The dog is man's best friend," and write down as many unusual and interesting supporting arguments as you can think of, ones that would really stick. Arrange your items in order of increasing interest.

6. Arrange the following points in order of ascending interest, and in a *pro-con* structure, adding necessary *but*'s and *of course*'s and so forth, and other intermediate points of your own:

The United Nations has not prevented war.
The United Nations provides a safety valve for international pressures.
The United Nations gives small nations a necessary sense of prestige.
The United Nations should include Red China.
The large nations dominate the United Nations.

7. Write an outline of a comparative argument. State your thesis; then simply list your points in order of increasing interest, phrasing them in the general pattern of "Football is good, but baseball is better."

3. Paragraphs

The Standard Paragraph

A PARAGRAPH is a structural convenience—a building-block to get firmly in mind. I mean the standard, central paragraph, setting aside for the moment the peculiarly shaped beginning paragraph and ending paragraph. You build the bulk of your essay with standard paragraphs, with blocks of concrete ideas, and they must fit smoothly. But they must also remain as perceptible parts, to rest your reader's eye and mind. Indeed, the paragraph originated, among the Greeks, as a resting place and place-finder, being first a mere mark (*graphos*) in the margin alongside (*para*) an unbroken sheet of handwriting—the proofreader's familiar ¶. You have heard that a paragraph is a single idea, and this is true. But so is a word, usually; and so is a sentence, sometimes. It seems best, after all, to think of a paragraph as something you use for your reader's convenience, rather than as some granitic form laid down by molten logic.

The writing medium determines the size of the paragraph. Your average longhand paragraph may look the same size to you as a typewritten one, and both may seem the same size as a paragraph in a book. But the printed page might show your handwritten paragraph so short as to be embarrassing, and your typewritten paragraph barely long enough for decency. Handwriting plus typewriting plus insecurity equals inadequate paragraphs. Your first impulse may be to write little paragraphs, often only a sentence to each. If so, you are not yet writing in any medium at all.

Journalists, of course, are habitually one-sentence paragraphers.

The narrowness of the newspaper column makes a sentence look like a paragraph, and narrow columns and short paragraphs serve the rapid transit for which newspapers are designed. A paragraph from a book might fill a whole newspaper column with solid lead. It would have to be broken—paragraphed—for the reader's convenience. On the other hand, a news story on the page of a book would look like a gap-toothed comb, and would have to be consolidated for the reader's comfort.

Plan for the big paragraph. Imagine yourself writing for print, but in a book, not a newspaper. Force yourself to four or five sentences at least, visualizing your paragraphs as about all of a size. Think of them as identical rectangular frames to be filled. This will allow you to build with orderly blocks, to strengthen your feel for structure. Since the beginner's problem is usually one of thinking of things to say rather than of trimming the overgrowth, you can do your filling-out a unit at a time, always thinking up one or two sentences more to fill the customary space. You will probably be repetitive and wordy at first—this is our universal failing—but you will soon learn to fill your paragraph with clean and interesting details. You will get to feel a kind of constructional rhythm as you find yourself coming to a resting place at the end of your customary paragraphic frame. Once accustomed to a five-sentence frame, say, you can then begin to vary the length for structural and rhetorical emphasis, letting a good idea swell out beyond the norm, or bringing a particular point home in a paragraph short and sharp.

Find a topic sentence. Looked at as a convenient structural frame, the paragraph reveals a further advantage. Like the essay itself, it has a beginning, a middle, and an end. The beginning and the end are usually each one sentence long, and the middle gets you smoothly from one to the other. Since, like the essay, the paragraph flows through time, its last sentence is the most emphatic. This is your home punch. The first sentence holds the next most emphatic place. It will normally be your *topic sentence*, stating the small thesis of a miniature essay, something like this:

> **Jefferson believed in democracy because of his fearless belief in reason. He knew that reason was far from perfect, but he also**

knew that it was the best faculty we have. He knew that it was better than all the frightened and angry intolerances with which we fence off our own back yards at the cost of injustice. Thought must be free. Discussion must be free. Reason must be free to range among the widest possibilities. Even the opinion we hate, and have reasons for believing wrong, we must leave free so that reason can operate on it, so that we advertise our belief in reason and demonstrate a faith unafraid of the consequences—because we know that the consequences will be right. Freedom is really not the aim and end of Jeffersonian democracy: freedom is the means by which democracy can rationally choose justice for all.

If your topic sentence covers everything within your paragraph, you are using your paragraphs with maximum effect, leading your reader into your community block by block. If your end sentences bring him briefly to rest, he will know where he is and appreciate it. That is the standard paragraph. But you build your beginning paragraph in reverse order.

Beginning Paragraphs: The Funnel

State your thesis at the END of your beginning paragraph. Your beginning paragraph must contain your main idea, and present it to best advantage. Its topic sentence is also the *thesis sentence* of your entire essay. The clearest and most emphatic place for your thesis sentence is at the *end*—not at the beginning—of the beginning paragraph. If you put it first, you will have to repeat some version of it as you bring your beginning paragraph to a close. If you put it in the middle, the reader will very likely take something else as your main point, probably whatever the last sentence contains. The inevitable psychology of interest, as you move your reader through your first paragraph and into your essay, urges you to put your thesis last—in the last sentence of your beginning paragraph.

Think of your beginning paragraph, then, not as a frame to be filled, but as a funnel. Start wide and end narrow:

BROAD GENERALIZATION

THESIS

If, for instance, you wished to show that Mozart's superiority lay in revivifying musical commonplaces, you should start some small distance back from that point. You could start almost anywhere, but with some innocuous and peaceable proposition: "Mozart is one of the great names in music," or "Everyone likes the familiar," or "Music undoubtedly has charms for everyone." Your opening line, in other words, should be innocent, acceptable, and inoffensive, something to which all readers would agree without rise in blood pressure. (Antagonize and startle if you wish, but beware of losing your friends and of making your thesis an anticlimax.) Therefore: broad and genial. From the opening pleasant generalization you move progressively down to particulars. You narrow down: from all music, to eighteenth-century music, to eighteenth-century musical commonplaces, to Haydn and Mozart, to Mozart, to "the surprising turn and depth Mozart gives to the most conventional musical phrases" (your thesis). Your paragraph might run, from broad to narrow, something like this:

> All people, even the tone-deaf, like some kind of music, and the old and familiar is usually the most appealing. For modern listeners, the eighteenth century usually represents this kind of comfortable familiarity—undemanding, pleasant, and commonplace. Indeed, eighteenth-century music developed and used a number of musical commonplaces. Composers were all working in the same style, tonality, and phraseology, and they often sound very much alike. Many people will say, for instance, that Haydn and his musical heir, Mozart, are as like as two peas. But Mozart

far outdid his master. He used Haydn's conventions, but in those very conventions he found new expressive power. Indeed, Mozart's genius may be said to lie in his ability to make the commonplace continually surprising, fresh, and deep. We get the old with the ever surprisingly new.

Now, that paragraph turned out a little different from what I anticipated. I even violated my rule of placing the thesis last. I went one sentence further for emphasis and for coherence with the first sentence. But it illustrates the funnel, from the broad and general to the one particular point, which is the main idea, the thesis. Here is another example:

Everyone likes a garden, even if for nothing more than a look in driving by. As man put down paving stones and discovered cement, he also discovered that he needed a little space for something green and growing. However much he may like the comfort of a house and the security of a city, he cannot completely cut himself off from nature. Even the tenement dweller will devise his window box. And suburbia represents a kind of mass movement into the lawns and shrubbery. But few of the onlookers ever realize how much work a garden can be.

MIDDLE PARAGRAPHS

Make your middle paragraphs full, and use transitions. The middle paragraph is the standard paragraph, the little essay in itself, with its own little beginning and little end. But it must also declare its allegiance to the paragraphs immediately before and after it. Each topic sentence must somehow hook onto the paragraph above it, must include some transitional word or phrase. You may simply repeat a word from the sentence that ended the paragraph just above. You may bring down a thought left slightly hanging in air: "His ideas are different" might be a tremendously economical topic sentence with automatic transition. Or you may get from one paragraph to the next by the usual steppingstones, like *but, however, nevertheless, therefore, indeed, of course.* One brief transitional touch in your topic sentence is usually sufficient.

The topic sentences in each of the following three paragraphs by Mr. W. H. Auden contain neat transitions. I have just used an old stand-by myself: repeating the words *topic sentence* from the close of the preceding paragraph. Mr. Auden, a distinguished poet, is accepting the chair of Professor of Poetry at Oxford. He has been explaining how accidental and diverse a growing poet's background is. He now moves into the subject of formal education, with a *then* making the transition from general diversity to academic diversity. In the next paragraph, *But this* does the trick; in the last, *however*. The paragraphs are nearly the same length, all cogent, clear, and full. No one-sentence paragraphing here, no gaps, but all a lively, orderly progression:

It is hardly surprising, then, if a young poet seldom does well in his examinations. If he does, then either he is also a scholar in the making, or he is a very good boy indeed. A medical student knows that he must study anatomy in order to become a doctor, so he has a reason for study. A future scholar has a reason, because he knows more or less what he wants to know. But there is nothing a would-be poet knows he has to know. He is at the mercy of the immediate moment because he has no concrete reason for not yielding to its demands, and, for all he knows, surrendering to his immediate desire may turn out later to have been the best thing he could have done. His immediate desire can even be to attend a lecture. I remember one I attended, delivered by Professor Tolkien. I do not remember a single word he said, but at a certain point he recited, and magnificently, a long passage of *Beowulf*. I was spellbound. This poetry, I knew, was going to be my dish. I became willing, therefore, to work at Anglo-Saxon because, unless I did, I should never be able to read this poetry. I learned enough to read it, however sloppily, and Anglo-Saxon and Middle English poetry have been one of my strongest, most lasting influences.

But this was something which neither I nor anybody else could have foreseen. Again, what good angel lured me into Blackwell's one afternoon and, from such a wilderness of volumes, picked out for me the essays of William Paton Ker? No other critic whom I have subsequently read could have granted me the same vision of a kind of literary All Souls Night in which the dead, the living, and the unborn writers of every age and in every tongue were seen as engaged upon a common noble and civilizing task. No other could have so instantaneously aroused in me a fascination with prosody, which I have never lost.

You must not imagine, however, that being a bad boy is all fun. During my three years as an undergraduate, I had a high old time, I made some lifelong friends, and I was more unhappy than

I have ever been before or since. I might or might not be wasting my time—only the future would show—I was certainly wasting my parents' money. Nor must you think that, because he fails to study, a young poet looks down his nose at all the scholarly investigations going on around him. Unless he is very young indeed, he knows that if it had not been for scholars working themselves blind copying and collating manuscripts, many poems would be unavailable, including those of Catullus, and many others full of lines that made no sense. Nor has the invention of printing made editors unnecessary. Lucky the poet whose collected works are not full of misprints.*

End Paragraphs: The Inverted Funnel

Reassert your thesis.   If the beginning paragraph is a funnel, the end paragraph is a funnel upside down: the thought starts moderately narrow—it is more or less the thesis you have had all the time—and then pours out broader and broader implications and finer emphases. The end paragraph reiterates, summarizes, and emphasizes with decorous fervor. This is your last chance. This is what your reader will carry away—and if you can carry *him* away, so much the better. All within decent intellectual bounds, of course. You are the man of reason still, but the man of reason surcharged with conviction, sure of his idea and sure of its importance.

The last paragraph conveys a sense of assurance and repose, of business completed. Its topic sentence should be some version of your original thesis sentence, since the end paragraph is the exact structural opposite and complement of the beginning one. Its transitional word or phrase is often one of finality or summary—*then, finally, thus,* and *so:*

> Mozart's commonplaces, then, are like proverbs—old truths in surprisingly new situations.
> And so the beautiful garden grew more problems than roses.

The paragraph would then proceed to expand and elaborate this revived thesis. We would get an earnest epitome of Mozart's particular beauty, and of his ultimate quality and value; we would get an amusing sense of the gardener's endless buying of spray and

---

* W. H. Auden, "Making and Judging Poetry," *Atlantic Monthly,* January, 1957, pp. 46–47.

fertilizer, his despair in trying to sweep back the waves of weeds. One rule of thumb: the longer the paper, the more specific the summary of the points you have made. A short paper will need no specific summary of your points at all; the renewed thesis and its widening of implications are sufficient.

Here is an end paragraph by Sir James Jeans. His transitional word is *Thus*. His thesis was that the sky is blue because the short blue light waves are diffused by dust and the long red ones are not:

> **Thus the different constituents of sunlight are treated in different ways as they struggle through the earth's atmosphere. A wave of blue light may be scattered by a dust particle, and turned out of its course. After a time a second dust particle again turns it out of its course, and so on, until finally it enters our eyes by a path as zigzag as that of a flash of lightning. Consequently the blue waves of the sunlight enter our eyes from all directions. And that is why the sky looks blue.**

Here is the end paragraph of Auden's Oxford address. His transitional word is *Whatever*, since he has been talking about the different kinds of poems that can express a poet's "sacred encounters of his imagination." His thesis was that there is something both unexpected and mysterious about a poet's arrival at a poem:

> **Whatever its actual content and overt interest, every poem is rooted in imaginative awe. Poetry can do a hundred and one things, delight, sadden, disturb, amuse, instruct—it may express every possible shade of emotion, and describe every conceivable kind of event, but there is only one thing that all poetry must do: it must praise all it can for being and for happening.***

Here is an end paragraph by Professor Richard Hofstadter. His transitional word is *intellectuals*, carried over from the preceding paragraph. His thesis was that intellectuals should not abandon their defense of intellectual and spiritual freedom, as they have tended to do, under pressure to conform:

> **This world will never be governed by intellectuals—it may rest assured. But *we* must be assured, too, that intellectuals will not be altogether governed by this world, that they maintain their piety, their longstanding allegiance to the world of spiritual values to which they should belong. Otherwise there will be no intellec-**

* Auden, p. 52.

tuals, at least not above ground. And societies in which the intellectuals have been driven underground, as we have had occasion to see in our own time, are societies in which even the anti-intellectuals are unhappy.

THE WHOLE ESSAY

The Keyhole. You have now discovered the main ingredients of a good essay. You have learned to find and to sharpen your thesis, to give your essay that all-important argumentative edge. You have learned to arrange your points in order of increasing interest, and you have practiced disposing of the opposition in a *pro-con* structure. You have seen that your beginning paragraph should look like a funnel, working from broad generalization to thesis. You have tried your hand at middle paragraphs, which are almost like little essays with their own beginnings and ends. And finally, you have learned that your last paragraph should work like an inverted funnel, broadening and embellishing your thesis. You are ready to open the door to good writing; the keyhole * on page 25 will provide you with a picture of the way your completed essay should look.

EXERCISES

1. Write three beginning paragraphs of five or six sentences each, working down in each to some such terse thesis as one of these: "Without health there is nothing." "Reason is best." "Everything is relative." "Always prepare for the worst." "Live for the day." "Worry is good."

2. Write ten topic sentences for end paragraphs, each with a different transitional tag, as in these examples: "Ill health, *then,* darkens every prospect and discolors every thought." "It is clear, *therefore,* that ill health has produced more truth and more beauty—more art, more literature, more music, and a good share of philosophy, history, invention, and scientific insight—than have all the muscles in all outdoors." "One can, *in the last analysis,* live only the present moment."

* Mrs. Fran Measley of Santa Barbara, California, has devised for her students of writing a mimeographed sheet to accompany my discussion of structure and paragraphing—to help them to visualize my points, through a keyhole, as it were. The Keyhole became so widely used in Santa Barbara that many teachers were surprised to learn that it was not in the book. I am grateful to Mrs. Measley to be able now to include it.

THE KEYHOLE

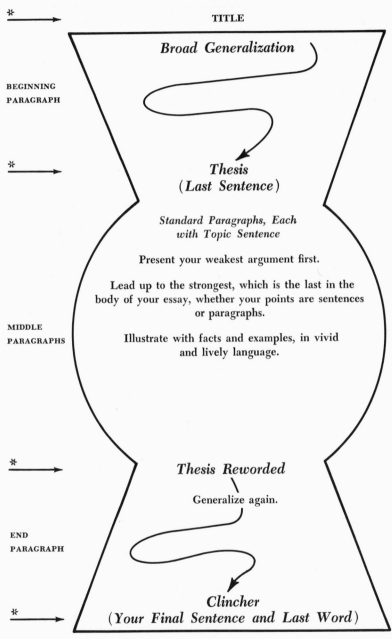

TITLE

Broad Generalization

BEGINNING
PARAGRAPH

Thesis
(*Last Sentence*)

*Standard Paragraphs, Each
with Topic Sentence*

Present your weakest argument first.

Lead up to the strongest, which is the last in the
body of your essay, whether your points are sentences
or paragraphs.

Illustrate with facts and examples, in vivid
and lively language.

MIDDLE
PARAGRAPHS

Thesis Reworded

Generalize again.

END
PARAGRAPH

Clincher
(*Your Final Sentence and Last Word*)

° Focal points

3. Write three unrelated middle paragraphs, about 200 words each. Make the topic sentences cover the contents, and give each topic sentence some transitional touch: "Fly fishing *is different.*" "*But* Judaism acknowledges man as a social being." "Kennedy *also* had his blind side."

4. Write an essay with uniform paragraphs, each about 125 words long, each, after a good beginning paragraph with a thesis, having a good sharp topic sentence—and don't forget the end.

5. Write a three-paragraph essay, then expand it into a five-paragraph essay, keeping the same beginning paragraph and end paragraph, and hand in both versions.

4. Writing Good Sentences

ALL THIS TIME you have been writing sentences, as naturally as breathing, and perhaps with as little variation. Now for a close look at the varieties of the sentence. Some varieties can be shaggy and tangled indeed. But they are all offshoots of the simple active sentence, the basic English genus *John hit Joe,* with action moving straight from subject through verb to object.

This subject-verb-object sentence can be infinitely grafted and contorted, but there are really only two general varieties of it: (1) the "loose, or strung-along," in Aristotle's phrase, and (2) the periodic. English naturally runs "loose." Our thoughts are by nature strung along from subject through verb to object, with whatever comes to mind simply added as it comes—a word order happily acquired from French as a result of the Norman Conquest. But we can also use the periodic sentence characteristic of our German and Latin ancestry, a sentence in which ideas hang in the air like girders until all interconnections are locked by the final word: *John, the best student in the class, the tallest and most handsome, hit Joe.*

So we have two varieties of the English sentence, partly because its old Germanic oak was first limbered by French and then cured by Latin, but mostly because (as Aristotle observed of Greek) the piece-by-piece and the periodic species simply represent two ways of thought: the first, the natural stringing of thoughts as they come; the second, the more careful contrivance of emphasis and suspense.

THE SIMPLE SENTENCE

Use the simple active sentence, loosely periodic. Your best sentences will be hybrids of the loose and the periodic. First, learn

27

to use active verbs (*John* HIT *Joe*), which will keep you within the simple active pattern with all parts showing (subject-verb-object), as opposed to verbs in the passive voice (*Joe* WAS HIT *by John*), which throw your sentences into the shade. Then learn to give your native strung-along sentence a touch of periodicity and suspense.

Any change in normal order can give you unusual emphasis, as when you move the object ahead of the subject:

> **That I like.**
> **The house itself she hated, but the yard was grand.**
> **Nature I loved; and next to Nature, Art.**
> **The manuscript, especially, he treasured.**

You can vary the subject-verb-object pattern more gently by interruptive words and phrases, so that the meaning gathers excitement from the delay. The *especially* does more for the manuscript than the words themselves could manage: the phrase postpones the already postponed subject and predicate. Put the phrase last, and the emphasis fades considerably; the speaker grows a little remote: "The manuscript he treasured, especially." Put the sentence in normal order—"He especially treasured the manuscript"—and we are, in fact, back to normal.

We expect our ideas one at a time, in normal succession—*John hit Joe*—and with anything further added, in proper sequence, at the end—*a real haymaker.* Change this fixed way of thinking, and you immediately put your reader on the alert for something unusual. Consequently, some of your best sentences will be simple active ones sprung wide with phrases coloring subject, verb, object, or all three, in various ways. You may, for instance, effectively complicate the subject:

> **A long black car, with two expressionless men in front, nobody in back, and muddy license plates conspicuous against its emphatic gloss, rolled softly by.**
> **To come all this way, to arrive after dark, and then to find the place locked and black as ink was almost unbearable.**

Or the verb:

> **He made his way, carefully at first, then confidently, then with reckless steps, along the peak of the smoldering roof.**
> **A good speech usually begins quietly, proceeds sensibly, gathers**

momentum, and finally moves even the most indifferent audience.

Or the object:

> She finally wrote the paper, a long desperate perambulation with-
> out beginning or end, without any guiding idea—without, in
> fact, much of an idea at all.
>
> His notebooks contain marvelous comments on the turtle in his back
> yard, the flowers and weeds, the great elm by the drive, the
> road, the earth, the stars, and the men and women of the village.

These are some of the infinite possibilities in the simple active sentence as it delays and stretches and heightens the ordinary ex-
pectations of subject-verb-object.

COMPOUND AND COMPLEX SENTENCES

Learn the difference between compound and complex sentences.
You make a compound sentence by linking together simple sentences with a coordinating conjunction (*and, but, or, nor, yet*) or
with a colon or a semicolon. You make a complex one by hooking
lesser sentences onto the main sentence with *that, which, who,* or
one of the many other subordinating connectives like *although, because, where, when, after, if.* The compound sentence *coordinates,*
treating everything on the same level; the complex *subordinates,*
putting everything else somewhere below its one main self-suf-
ficient idea. The compound links ideas one after the other, as in
the basic simple sentence; the complex is a simple sentence delayed
and elaborated by clauses instead of merely by phrases. The compound represents the strung-along way of thinking; the complex
represents the periodic.

Avoid simple-minded compounds.   Essentially the compound sentence *is* simple-minded, a set of clauses on a string—a child's description of a birthday party, for instance: "We got paper hats and
we pinned the tail on the donkey and we had chocolate ice cream
and Randy sat on a piece of cake and I won third prize." *And . . .
and . . . and.*

But this way of thinking is necessary, even in postgraduate regions. It is always useful simply for pacing off related thoughts, and
for breaking the staccato of simple statement. It often briskly

connects cause and effect: "The clock struck one, and down he run." "The solipsist relates all knowledge to his own being, and the demonstrable commonwealth of human nature dissolves before his dogged timidity." The *and* can link causes with all sorts of different effects and speed, can bring in the next clause as a happy after-thought or a momentous consequence. Since the compound sentence is built on the most enduring of colloquial patterns—the simple sequence of things said as they occur to the mind—it has the pace, the immediacy, and the dramatic effect of talk. Hemingway, for instance, often gets all the numb tension of a shell-shocked mind by reducing his character's thoughts all to one level, in sentences something like this: "It was a good night and I sat at a table and . . . and . . . and . . . ."

With *but* and *or,* the compound sentence becomes more thoughtful. The mind is at work, turning its thought first one way then another, meeting the reader's objections by stating them. With semicolon and colon (or, if the clauses are very short, with comma), the compound grows more sophisticated still:

> **Men demand the most from themselves; women demand.**
> **I came, I saw, I conquered.**
> **Economic theorists assume a common man: he commonly wants more than he can supply.**

Think of the compound sentence in terms of its conjunctions— the words that yoke its clauses—and of the accompanying punctuation. Here are three basic groups of conjunctions that will help you sort out and punctuate your compound thoughts.

GROUP I. *The three common coordinating conjunctions:* and, but, *and* or (nor). *Put a comma before each.*

> **I like her, and I don't mind saying so.**
> **Art is long, but life is short.**
> **Win this point, or the game is lost.**

GROUP II. *Conjunctive adverbs:* therefore, moreover, however, nevertheless, consequently, furthermore. *Put a semicolon before, a comma after, each.*

> **Nations indeed seem to have a kind of biological span like the ages of man himself, from rebellious youth, through caution, to decay; consequently, predictions of doom are not uncommon.**

G R O U P I I I . *Some in-betweeners—yet, still, so—which sometimes take a comma, sometimes a semicolon, depending on your pace and emphasis.*

We long for the good old days, yet we never include the disadvantages.

Man longs for the good old days; yet he rarely takes into account the inaccuracy of human memory.

The preparation had been halfhearted and hasty, so the meeting was wretched.

Rome declined into the pleasures of its circuses and couches; so the tough barbarians conquered.

Learn to subordinate. You probably write compound sentences almost without thinking. But the subordinations of the complex usually require some thought. You must pick your most important idea. You must change the thoughtless *co*ordination of mere sequence into various forms of *sub*ordination. The birthday sentence, then, might come out something like this:

After paper hats and chocolate ice cream, after Randy's sitting on a piece of cake and everyone's pinning the tail on the donkey, I WON FIRST PRIZE.

You do the trick with connectives—with any word, like *after* in the sentence above, indicating time, place, cause, or other qualification:

If he tries, *if* he fails, HE IS STILL GREAT *because* his spirit is unbeaten.

You daily achieve subtler levels of subordination with the three relative pronouns *that, which, who,* and with the conjunction *that. That, which,* and *who* connect thoughts so closely related as to seem almost equal, but actually each tucks a clause (subject-and-verb) into some larger idea:

The car, *which* runs perfectly, is not worth selling.

The car *that* runs perfectly is worth keeping.

He thought *that* the car would run forever.

He thought [*that* omitted but understood] the car would run forever.

But the subordinating conjunctions and adverbs (*although, if, because, since, until, where, when, as if, so that*) really put subordinates in their places. Look at *when* in this sentence of E. B. White's:

> Next morning *when* the first light came into the sky and the spar-
> rows stirred in the trees, *when* the cows rattled their chains and
> the rooster crowed and the early automobiles went whispering
> along the road, Wilbur awoke and looked for Charlotte.

Here the simple *when,* used only twice, has regimented five subordinate clauses, all of equal rank, into their proper station below
that of the main clause, "Wilbur awoke and looked for Charlotte."
You can vary the ranking intricately and still keep it straight, if
the mood should take you:

> *Although* some claim *that* time is an illusion, *because* we have no
> absolute chronometer, *although* the mind cannot effectively grasp
> time, *because* the mind itself is a kind of timeless presence almost
> oblivious to seconds and hours, *although* the time of our solar
> system may be only an instant in the universe at large, WE STILL
> CANNOT QUITE DENY *that* some progression of universal time is
> passing over us, if only we could measure it.

Complex sentences are at their best really simple sentences
gloriously delayed and elaborated. The following beautiful and
elaborate sentence from the Book of Common Prayer is all built
on the simple sentence "draw near":

> Ye who do truly and earnestly repent you of your sins, and are
> in love and charity with your neighbors, and intend to lead a new
> life, following the commandments of God, and walking from hence-
> forth in his holy ways, draw near with faith, and take this holy
> sacrament to your comfort, and make your humble confession to
> Almighty God, devoutly kneeling.

Even a short sentence may be complex, attaining a remarkably
varied suspense. Notice how the simple statement "I allowed myself" is skillfully elaborated in this sentence by the late Wolcott
Gibbs of *The New Yorker:*

> Twice in my life, for reasons that escape me now, though I'm
> sure they were discreditable, I allowed myself to be persuaded
> that I ought to take a hand in turning out a musical comedy.

Once you glimpse the complex choreography possible within the
dimensions of the simple sentence, you are on your way to developing a prose capable of turns and graceful leaps, one with a kind of

intellectual health that, no matter what the subject or mood, is always on its toes.

Try for still closer connections: modify. Your subordinating *if*'s and *when*'s have really been modifying—that is, limiting—the things you have attached them to. But there is a smoother way. It is an adjectival sort of thing, a shoulder-to-shoulder operation, a neat trick with no need for shouting, a stone to a stone with no need for mortar. You simply put clauses and phrases up against a noun, instead of attaching them with a subordinator. This sort of modification includes the following constructions, all using the same close masonry: (1) appositives, (2) relatives understood, (3) adjectives-with-phrase, (4) participles, (5) absolutes.

A P P O S I T I V E S . Those phrases about shoulders and tricks and stones, above, are all in apposition with *sort of thing*, and they are grammatically subordinate to it. The phrases are nevertheless nearly coordinate and interchangeable. They are compressions of a series of sentences ("It is an adjectival sort of thing. It is a neat trick . . . ," and so forth) set side by side, "stone to stone." Mere contact does the work of the verb *is* and its subject *it*. English often does the same with subordinate clauses, omitting the *who is* or *which is* and putting the rest directly into apposition. "The William who is the Conqueror" becomes "William the Conqueror." "The Jack who is the heavy hitter" becomes "Jack the heavy hitter." These, incidentally, are called "restrictive" appositions, because they restrict to a particular designation the nouns they modify, setting this William and this Jack apart from all others (with no separating commas). Similarly, you can make nonrestrictive appositives from nonrestrictive clauses, clauses that simply add information (between commas). "Smith, who is a man to be reckoned with, . . ." becomes "Smith, a man to be reckoned with, ..." "Jones, who is our man in Liverpool, . . ." becomes "Jones, our man in Liverpool, ..." Restrictive or nonrestrictive, close contact makes your point. You glow with the pleasures of economy and fitness.

R E L A T I V E S   U N D E R S T O O D . You can often achieve the same economy, as I have already hinted, by omitting any kind of relative and its verb, thus gaining a compression both colloquial and classic:

A compression [that is] both colloquial and classic . . . .
The specimens [that] he had collected . . . .
The girl [whom] he [had] left behind . . . .

But be careful after verbs of feeling and seeing; omitting *that* may lead to confusion: "She felt his ears were too big." "He saw her nose was too small."

ADJECTIVES-WITH-PHRASE. This construction is also appositive and adjectival. It is elegant, neat, and useful:

> The law was passed, *thick with provisions and codicils, heavy with implications.*
> There was the lake, *smooth in the early air.*

PARTICIPLES. Participles—verbs acting as adjectives—are extremely supple subordinators. Consider these three coordinate sentences:

> He finally reached home. He discovered how tired he was. He went to bed without reading his mail.

Change the main verbs into present participles, and you can subordinate any two of the sentences to the other (so long as you still make sense), economizing on excess *He*'s, balancing incidentals, and emphasizing the main point. You simply use the participles as adjectives to modify the subject *he:*

> Finally *reaching* home, *discovering* how tired he was, he went to bed . . . .

The past participle has the same adjectival power:

> Dead to the world, *wrapped* in sweet dreams, *untroubled* by bills, he slept till noon.

You will appreciate how like the adjective is the participle when you notice that *dead,* in the sentence above, is in fact an adjective, and that the participles operate exactly as it does.

Beware of dangling participles. They may trip you, as they have tripped others. The participle, with its adjectival urge, may grab the first noun that comes along, with shocking results:

> Bowing to the crowd, the bull caught him unawares.
> Observing quietly from the bank, the beavers committed several errors in judgment.

Squandering everything on beer, the money was never paid.
By bending low, the snipers could not see the retreating squad.
Tired and discouraged, half the lawn was still uncut.
What we need is a list of teachers broken down alphabetically.

Simply move the participle next to its intended noun or pronoun; you will have to supply this word if inadvertence or the passive voice has omitted it entirely. You may also save the day by changing a present participle to a past:

Observed quietly from the bank, the beavers . . . .
Squandered on beer, the money . . . .

Or you may move to ultimate sophistication by giving your participle a subject of its own within the phrase:

Every cent squandered on beer, the money was never paid.

Here is a sentence from Jane Austen's *Persuasion* that illustrates the adjectival and subordinating power of the participle—*delighted* twice modifying *She* and subordinating everything to the one basic four-word clause that begins the sentence:

She always watched them as long as she could, delighted to fancy she understood what they might be talking of, as they walked along in happy independence, or equally delighted to see the Admiral's hearty shake of the hand when he encountered an old friend, and observe their eagerness of conversation when occasionally forming into a little knot of the navy, Mrs. Croft looking as intelligent and keen as any of the officers around her.

This sentence ends so gracefully because, with the phrase *Mrs. Croft looking*, it achieves the ultimate in participial perfection— the ablative absolute.

A B S O L U T E S . The absolute phrase has a great potential of polished economy. Many an absolute is simply a prepositional phrase with the preposition dropped:

He ran up the stairs, [with] *a bouquet of roses under his arm,* and rang the bell.
He walked slowly, [with] *his gun at the ready.*

But the ablative absolute is the supreme sophisticate of subordination. *Ablative* means "removed," and the ablative absolute is absolutely removed from grammatical connection with the main clause, modifying only by proximity. If you have suffered the rudiments of Latin, you will probably remember this construction as some kind of brusque condensation, something like *"The road completed,* Caesar moved his camp." But it survives in the best of circles. Somewhere E. B. White admits to feeling particularly good one morning, just having brought off an especially fine ablative absolute. The construction does have tone. And it is actually more common than you may suppose. A recent newspaper article stated that "the Prince has fled the country, *his hopes of a negotiated peace shattered."* The *hopes shattered* pattern (noun plus participle) marks the ablative absolute. The idea might have been more conventionally subordinated: "since his hopes were shattered" or "with his hopes shattered." But the ablative absolute accomplishes the subordination with economy and style.

Take a regular subordinate clause: *"When* the road *was* completed." Cut the subordinator and the finite verb. You now have an ablative absolute, a phrase that stands absolutely alone, shorn of both its connective *when* and its full predication *was: "The road completed,* Caesar moved his camp." Basically a noun and a participle, or noun and adjective, it is a kind of grammatical shorthand, a telegram: *ROAD COMPLETED CAESAR MOVED*—most said in fewest words, speed with high compression. This is its appeal and its power.

> The cat stopped, its *back arched,* its *eyes frantic.*
> The whole economy, *God willing,* soon will return to normal.
> *All things considered,* the plan would work.
> The *dishes washed,* the *baby bathed* and *asleep,* the last *ash tray emptied,* she could at last relax.

It is certainly a construction you should use with caution. It can sound exactly like a bad translation. But able writers come to it sooner or later, whether knowingly or through discovering for themselves the horsepower in a subordinate clause milled down to its absolute minimum of noun and participle, or noun and adjective, or even noun and noun. Hemingway uses it frequently. Here is one of the noun-noun variety at the end of a sentence about pistols in *To Have and Have Not:* ". . . their only *drawback the mess* they leave for relatives to clean up." And here are two noun-participle ones (*he playing* and *the death administered*), in a passage that will serve as a closing illustration of how a complex sentence can subordinate as many as 164 words to the 7 of its one main clause ("They will put up with mediocre work"):

> If the spectators know the matador is capable of executing a complete, consecutive series of passes with the muleta in which there will be valor, art, understanding and, above all, beauty and great emotion, THEY WILL PUT UP WITH MEDIOCRE WORK, cowardly work, disastrous work because they have the hope sooner or later of seeing the complete faena; the faena that takes a man out of himself and makes him feel immortal while it is proceeding, that gives him an ecstasy, that is, while momentary, as profound as any religious ecstasy; moving all the people in the ring together and increasing in emotional intensity as it proceeds, carrying the bullfighter with it, he playing on the crowd through the bull and being moved as it responds in a growing ecstasy of ordered, formal, passionate, increasing disregard for death that leaves you, when it is over, and the death administered to the animal that has made it possible, as empty, as changed, and as sad as any major emotion will leave you.*

PARALLEL CONSTRUCTION

Use parallels wherever you can. Hemingway's 171-word sentence could not have held together without parallel construction, the masonry of syntax. No complex sentence can sustain a very long arch without it. Actually, Hemingway's "that is" after "ecstasy" makes a false parallel, throwing his arch briefly out of line (he should have used "which is" or something like "an ecstasy as profound, though momentary, as any . . ."). You have also seen examples of parallel ranking in White's *when* sentence (on p. 32) and in the sentence that followed, dealing with time. The sentence about the cat and the one about the relaxing housewife (on p. 36) have shown you ablative absolutes laid parallel.

Parallel masonry can be very simple. Any word will seek its own kind, noun to noun, adjective to adjective, infinitive to infinitive. The simplest series of things automatically runs parallel:

shoes and ships and sealing wax
I came, I saw, I conquered
to be or not to be

---

* *Death in the Afternoon* (New York: Scribner's, 1932), pp. 206–7.

a dull, dark, and soundless day
mediocre work, cowardly work, disastrous work

But they very easily run out of parallel too, and this you must learn to prevent. The last item especially may slip out of line, as in this series: "friendly, kind, unobtrusive, and *a bore*" (boring). Your paralleling articles and prepositions should govern a series as a whole, or should accompany *every* item:

a hat, a cane, a pair of gloves, and a mustache
a hat, cane, pair of gloves, and mustache
by land, by sea, or by air
by land, sea, or air

Repeat your paralleling connectives. When your series consists of phrases or of clauses, you should repeat the preposition or conjunction introducing them, to ensure clarity:

By weeks of careful planning, *by* intelligence, *by* thorough training, and *by* a great deal of luck . . . .
Since all things are not equal, *since* consequences cannot be foreseen, *since* we live but a moment . . . .
He looked *for* clean fingernails and polished shoes, *for* an air of composure, and *for* a quick wit.

Watch the paralleling of pairs. Pairs should be pairs, not odds and ends. Notice how the faulty pairs in these sentences have been corrected:

She liked *the lawn and gardening* (the lawn and the garden).
They were all *athletic or big men on campus* (athletes or big men on campus).
He wanted *peace without being disgraced* (peace without dishonor).
He liked *to play well and winning before a crowd* (to play well and to win; playing well and winning).
She was *shy but an attractive girl* (shy but attractive).

Check your terms on both sides of your coordinating conjunctions (*and, but, or*) and see that they match:

Orientation week seems both worthwhile [adjective] and ~~a necessity~~
necessary [noun].

He prayed that they would leave and / that the telephone would not
ring.

Learn to use paralleling coordinators.   The first sentence above
has used one of a number of useful (and tricky) parallel constructions: *Both/and; either/or; not only/but also; not/but; first/sec-
ond/third; as well as.* This last one is exactly like *and,* a simple
link between two equivalents, but it often causes trouble:

**A person should take care of his physical self [noun] *as well
as* being [participle] able to read and write.**

Again, the pair should be matched: "his physical self as well as
his intellectual self," or "his physical self as well as his ability to
read and write"—though this second is still slightly unbalanced, in
rhetoric if not in grammar. The best cure would probably extend
the underlying antithesis, the basic parallel:

**A person should take care of his physical self as well as his in-
tellectual self, of his ability to survive as well as to read and write.**

With the *either-or*'s and the *not-only-but-also*'s you continue the
principle of pairing. The *either* and the *not only* are merely sign-
posts of what is coming: two equivalents linked by a coordinating
conjunction (*or* or *but*). Beware of putting the signs in the wrong
place—too soon for the turn.

(Either) he is↘an absolute piker or a fool.

(Neither) in↘time nor space . . . .

He (not only) likes↘the girl, but the family, too.

In these examples, the thought got ahead of itself, as in talk. Just
make sure that the word following each of the two coordinators
is of the same kind, preposition for preposition, article for article,
adjective for adjective—for even with signs well placed, the parallel can skid:

    The students are not only organizing [present participle] social
                               discussing
    activities, but also ~~are interested~~ [passive construction] ~~in~~ politi-
    cal questions.

Put identical parts in parallel places; fill in the blanks with the
same parts of speech: "not only _____ , but also _____ ." You similarly parallel the words following numerical coordinators:

> However variously he expressed himself, he unquestionably
> thought, first, *that* everyone could get ahead; second, *that*
> workers generally were paid more than they earned; and, third,
> *that* laws enforcing a minimum wage were positively undemo-
> cratic.
>
> For a number of reasons he decided (1) that he did not like it,
> (2) that she would not like it, (3) that they would be better off
> without it. [Note that the parentheses around the numbers oper-
> ate exactly as any parenthesis, and need no additional punctua-
> tion.]
>
> My objections are obvious: (1) it is unnecessary, (2) it costs
> too much, and (3) it won't work.

In parallels of this kind, *that* is usually the problem, since you
may easily, and properly, omit it when there is only one clause
and no confusion:

> . . . he unquestionably thought everyone could get ahead.

If second and third clauses occur, as your thought moves along,
you may have to go back and put up the first signpost:

>   that
> . . . he unquestionably thought / everyone could get ahead, that
> workers . . . , and that laws . . . .

    Enough of *that.* Remember simply that equivalent thoughts de-
mand parallel constructions. Notice the clear and massive strategy
in the following sentence from the concluding chapter of Freud's
last book, *An Outline of Psychoanalysis.* Freud is summing up not
only the previous discussion but the quintessence of his life's work.
He is pulling everything together in a single sentence. Each of the
parallel *which*-clauses gathers up, in proper order, an entire chapter
of his book (notice the parallel force in repeating *picture,* and the
summarizing dash):

The picture of an ego which mediates between the id and the external world, which takes over the instinctual demands of the former in order to bring them to satisfaction, which perceives things in the latter and uses them as memories, which, intent upon its self-preservation, is on guard against excessive claims from both directions, and which is governed in all its decisions by the injunctions of a modified pleasure principle—this picture actually applies to the ego only up to the end of the first period of childhood, till about the age of five.

Such precision is hard to match. This is what parallel thinking brings—balance and control and an eye for sentences that seem intellectual totalities, as if struck out all at once from the uncut rock. Francis Bacon also can seem like this (notice how he drops the verb after establishing his pattern):

For a crowd is not company, and faces are but a gallery of pictures, and talk but a tinkling cymbal, where there is no love.

Reading maketh a full man; conference a ready man; and writing an exact man.

And the balance can run from sentence to sentence through an entire passage, controlled not only by connectives repeated in parallel, but by whole phrases and sentences so repeated, as in this passage by Macaulay:

To sum up the whole: we should say that the aim of the Platonic philosophy was to exalt man into a god. The aim of the Baconian philosophy was to provide man with what he requires while he continues to be man. The aim of the Platonic philosophy was to raise us far above vulgar wants. The aim of the Baconian philosophy was to supply our vulgar wants. The former aim was noble; but the latter was attainable.

THE LONG AND SHORT OF IT

Your style will emerge once you can manage some length of sentence, some intricacy of subordination, some vigor of parallel, and some play of long against short, of amplitude against brevity. Try the very long sentence, and the very short. The best short sentences are meatiest:

> To be awake is to be alive.
> A stitch in time saves nine.
> The mass of men lead lives of quiet desperation.
> The more selfish the man, the more anguished the failure.

Experiment, too, with the fragment, trying to cut and place it clearly (usually at beginnings and ends of paragraphs) so as not to lead your reader to expect a full sentence, or to suspect a poor writer:

> But no more.
> First, a look behind the scenes.
> Again: the man of reason.
> No, not really.
> Enough of that.

The fragment is close to conversation. It is the laconic reply, the pointed afterthought, the quiet exclamation, the telling question.

The conversational flow between long and short makes a passage move. Study the subordinations, the parallels, and the play of short and long in this elegant passage of Virginia Woolf's—after you have read it once for sheer enjoyment. She is writing of Lord Chesterfield's famous letters to Philip Stanhope, his illegitimate son:

> But while we amuse ourselves with this brilliant nobleman and his views on life we are aware, and the letters owe much of their fascination to this consciousness, of a dumb yet substantial figure on the farther side of the page. Philip Stanhope is always there. It is true that he says nothing, but we feel his presence in Dresden, in Berlin, in Paris, opening the letters and poring over them and looking dolefully at the thick packets which have been accumulating year after year since he was a child of seven. He had grown into a rather serious, rather stout, rather short young man. He had a taste for foreign politics. A little serious reading was rather to his liking. And by every post the letters came—urbane, polished, brilliant, imploring and commanding him to learn to dance, to learn to carve, to consider the management of his legs, and to seduce a lady of fashion. He did his best. He worked very hard in the school of the Graces, but their service was too exacting. He sat down half-way up the steep stairs which lead to the glittering hall with all the mirrors. He could not do it. He failed in the House of Commons; he subsided into some small post in Ratisbon;

he died untimely. He left it to his widow to break the news which he had lacked the heart or the courage to tell his father—that he had been married all these years to a lady of low birth, who had borne him children.

The Earl took the blow like a gentleman. His letter to his daughter-in-law is a model of urbanity. He began the education of his grandsons . . . .*

Those are some sentences to copy. We immediately feel the rhythmic play of periodic and loose, parallel and simple, long and short. Such orchestration takes years of practice, but you can always begin.

E X E R C I S E S

1. Write a dozen short sentences that invert normal order for emphasis: "That I like."

2. Write a dozen simple sentences (make sure you have no subordinate clauses), four complicating the subject, four the verb, and four the object.

3. Write a dozen compound sentences, four with *and,* four with *but,* four with *or* (*nor*). Try to get as grand a feeling of consequence as possible: "Empires fall, and the saints come marching in."

4. Write a dozen compound sentences using conjunctive adverbs, on the pattern: "_____ ; therefore, _____ "—punctuated carefully with semicolon and comma.

5. List all the subordinators you can think of (*since, if, before,* etc.).

6. Write five sequences of three simple sentences on the pattern: "He finally reached home. He was tired. He went to bed." Then, changing verbs to participles, subordinate two of the sentences to the remaining one in each sequence.

7. To appreciate participial subordination, rewrite each of the following as a series of simple coordinate sentences, changing the participles into finite verbs and the principal adjectives into predicate adjectives ("They danced. They swayed . . . . Some were intense."):

> They danced, swaying in dim light, dreaming happily, some laughing, some intense, some even embarrassed and awkward, wishing but failing to join the dream completely.
> Fishing, hiking, playing cribbage, sometimes talking seri-

---

* *The Second Common Reader,* Harvest Books (New York: Harcourt, Brace, 1932), p. 81.

ously, sometimes merely sitting together in silence, they spent the last of summer.

He was every inch a soldier, clipped, tailored, polished, as if straight from a musical comedy.

His train already late, his money stolen, his hat gone, his plans upset from start to finish, he hoped desperately that he still had time.

Complicated, misleading, inadequate, and motivated by special interests, the bill deserved defeat.

8. Review the discussion of parallel coordinators on pp. 39–40. Then write two sentences apiece for each of the following sets of coordinators. Try different parts of speech, but keep your parallels true by filling the blanks in any one sentence with the same parts of speech.

both _____ and _____
either _____ or _____
not only _____ but also _____
(1) _____ , (2) _____ , (3) _____
_____ as well as _____

9. Write a dozen sentences with dangling participles, with a remedy for each.

10. Write a dozen sentences with ablative absolutes, six using present participles, six using past.

11. Now, write four 100-word sentences *with only one independent clause* in each, and with everything else subordinated.

12. Adjust or clarify the parallels in the following (taken from freshmen papers):

These men are not only cheating themselves, but also are banded together into crime syndicates which help to lower the character of the entire nation.

He stated two ways in which man could hope to continue survival. (1) World citizenship, or (2) destroying most of the inventions that man is uncertain of and go back to where we can understand ourselves and progress.

In this way not only the teacher needs to be concerned with the poorest student, but every class member helped.

A student follows not only a special course of training, but among his studies and social activities finds a liberal education.

Education is something that can't be taken for granted but instead requires serious thought.

When they go to church, it is only because they have to go and not of their own desire.

Many people argue that the so-called virtues of man belong
to the age of chivalry, and they do not apply to the present.

This is not only the case with the young voters of the United
States but also of the adult ones.

. . . an education which will not only embarrass her but
also is dangerous to a self-governing people.

Certain things are not actually taught in the classroom. They
are learning how to get along with others, to depend on
oneself, and managing one's own affairs.

Every time I sit down and attempt to read one of those interesting essays, or else studying German . . . .

Knowing Greek and Roman antiquity is not just learning to
speak their language but also their culture.

I think fraternities are sociable as well as the dormitories.

All the girls now intend to get married as well as having
families of three or four.

13. (a) In the following famous sentence of Bacon's, straighten the
faulty parallels and fill out all the phrasing implied by them:

Histories make men wise; poets witty; the mathematics subtle; natural philosophy deep; moral grave; logic and rhetoric able to contend.

(b) Now write five sentences on the Baconian pattern: "Jack
would eat no fat; his wife no lean; the old dog only soup . . . ; the
young . . . ."

14. Write an imitation, or a parody, of the following passage from
Samuel Johnson, matching him sentence for sentence and phrase for
phrase ("Of genius, that power which constitutes a ball player . . . ."
"Of glamour, that power which constitutes an actress . . . ."):

Of genius, that power which constitutes a poet; that quality without which judgement is cold and knowledge is inert;
that energy which collects, combines, amplifies, and animates
—the superiority must, with some hesitation, be allowed to
Dryden. It is not to be inferred that of this poetical vigour
Pope had only a little, because Dryden had more, for every
other writer since Milton must give place to Pope; and even
of Dryden it must be said that if he has brighter paragraphs,
he has not better poems. Dryden's performances were always
hasty, either excited by some external occasion, or extorted
by domestick necessity; he composed without consideration,
and published without correction. What his mind could supply at call, or gather in one excursion, was all that he sought,

and all that he gave. The dilatory caution of Pope enabled him to condense his sentiments, to multiply his images, and to accumulate all that study might produce, or chance might supply. If the flights of Dryden therefore are higher, Pope continues longer on the wing. If of Dryden's fire the blaze is brighter, of Pope's the heat is more regular and constant. Dryden often surpasses expectation, and Pope never falls below it. Dryden is read with frequent astonishment, and Pope with perpetual delight.

15. Write an imitation of the passage from Virginia Woolf on pages 42–43, aiming toward effective rhythms of short and long.

5. Correcting Bad Sentences

Now LET US contemplate evil—or at least the innocently awful, the bad habits that waste our words, fog our thoughts, and wreck our delivery. Our thoughts are naturally roundabout, our phrases naturally secondhand. Our satisfaction in merely getting something down on paper naturally blinds us to our errors and ineptitudes. Writing is devilish. It hypnotizes us into believing we have said what we meant, when our words actually say something else: "Every seat in the house was filled to capacity." Good sentences therefore come from constant practice in correcting the bad.

The general sin is wordiness. We put down the first thought that comes, we miss the best order, and we then need lengths of *is*'s, *of*'s, *by*'s, and *which*'s—words virtually meaningless in themselves—to wire our meaningful words together again. Look for the two or three words that carry your meaning; then see if you can't rearrange them to speak for themselves, cutting out all the little useless wirings:

> This is the young man who was elected to be president by the class. [The class elected this young man president. *7 words for 14*]

See if you can't promote a noun into a verb, and cut overlaps in meaning:

> Last week, the gold stampede in Europe reached near panic proportions. [Europe's gold rush almost *stampeded* last week. *7 words for 11*]

The basic cure is to count the words in any suspected sentence —and to make each word count. If you can rephrase to save even one word, your sentence will be clearer. And seek the active verb: *John* HIT *Joe.*

Avoid the passive voice. The passive voice drones like nothing under the sun, bringing active English to a standstill. Of course, it can, in a string of active sentences, give mere variety, although phrasal and clausal variations are better. It can also vary the emphasis; it too depends on inverting normal order. *Joe was hit by John* throws selective light on Joe, by inverting regular consequences and distinguishing him from all other unfortunates, and it gives John a certain dubious distinction too. The passive voice can also, if need be, eliminate the doer altogether: *Joe was hit.* ("I was sunk." "It was done.")

In fact, your meaning sometimes demands the passive voice; the agent may be better under cover—insignificant, or unknown, or mysterious. The active "Shrapnel hit him" seems to belie the uncanny impersonality of "He was hit by shrapnel." The broad forces of history similarly demand the passive: "The West was opened in 1848." Moreover, you may sometimes need the passive voice to place your true subject, the hero of the piece, where you can modify him conveniently: *Joe was hit by John, who, in spite of all . . . .* And sometimes it simply is more convenient: "This subject-verb-object sentence can be infinitely contorted." You can, of course, find a number of passive constructions in this book, which preaches against them, because they can also space out a thought that comes too fast and thick. In trying to describe periodic sentences, for instance (p. 27), I changed "until all interconnections lock in the final word" (active) to ". . . are locked by the final word" (passive). The *lock* seemed too tight, especially with *in,* and the locking seemed contrary to the way buildings *are built.* Yes, the passive has its uses.

But avoid it if you can. It is wordy and unclear. It liquidates and buries the active individual. Our massed and scientific society is so addicted to the passive voice that the individual writer must constantly alert himself against its drowsy, soporific pomp. The simple English sentence is active; it *moves* from subject through verb to object: "Smith laid the cornerstone on April 1." But because we must sound important, because the impersonal institution must be bigger than Smith, the historian writes "The cornerstone was laid on April 1," and Smith vanishes from the earth. The doer and the writer both—all traces of individuality, all human interest—disappear behind the elongated passive verb: *was laid* instead of *laid.* Committees always write this way, and the effect on academic writing, as the professor goes from committee to desk to classroom, is astounding. "It was moved that a meeting would be held," the secretary writes, to avoid pinning the rap on anybody. So writes the professor, so writes the student.

The passive voice puts excess words in a sentence. Its dullness derives as much from its extra wordage as from its impersonality. *Joe was hit by John* says no more than *John hit Joe,* but takes sixty-six per cent more words! The passive's inevitable *was* and *by* do nothing but connect; worse, all the *was*'s and *by*'s and *has been*'s actually get in the way of the words carrying the meaning, like underbrush slowing you down and hiding what you want to see.

The best way to prune is with the active voice, cutting the passive and its fungus as you go. Notice the effect on the following typical, and actual, samples:

Public concern *has* also *been given* a tremendous impetus *by* the findings of the Hoover Commission on the federal government, and "little Hoover" commissions to survey the organizational structure and functions of many state governments *have been established.* [In the federal government, the findings of the Hoover Commission *have* also greatly stimulated public concern, and many states *have established* "little Hoover" commissions to survey their governments. *28 words for 38*]

The algal mats *are made up of* the interwoven filaments of several genera. [The interwoven filaments of several genera *make up* the algal mats. *11 words for 13*]

Many of the remedies *would* probably *be shown to be* faith cures. [Many of the remedies *are* probably faith cures. *8 words for 12*]

Anxiety and emotional conflict *are lessened* when latency sets in. The total personality *is oriented* in a repressive, inhibitory fashion so as to maintain the barriers, and what Freud has called "psychic dams," against psychosexual impulses. [When latency sets in, anxiety and emotional conflict *subside.* The personality *inhibits* itself, maintaining its barriers—Freud's "psychic dams"—against psychosexual impulses. *22 words for 36*]

The passive voice, simply in its wordiness, is always a bit unclear even on the surface; but, if it eliminates the real subject of the verb, as it usually does, it is intrinsically unclear as well. "This passage has been selected because . . . ," the student will write, and the reader cannot tell who did the selecting. Does he mean that he, the writer, has picked it, or does he describe some process of natural or popular selection? We surmise he means himself, of course; but why doesn't he say so, and save a word, and avoid confusion? "I selected this passage because . . . ."

Any form of the verb *is* may reveal that you have a passive construction. Our language must use some form of *is* so frequently in stating that things *are* and in forming its compound verbs (*is falling, were playing*) that you should drop as many *is*'s and *was*'s as possible, simply to avoid monotony. But when they are—as they often are—signs of the passive voice, you can also avoid rigor mortis by replacing your *is*'s with active verbs, along with their true subjects, the real doers of the action.

To be, itself, frequently ought not to be:

He seems [to be] upset about something.
She considered him [to be] perfect.
This appears [to be] difficult.

Similarly, many a *which, that, who,* and *whom* may depart, and good riddance:

The rule [which] the committee favors . . . .
I think [that] he should go.
The man [whom] I respect . . . .

Above all, keep your sentences awake by not putting them into those favorite stretchers of the passivists, *There is . . . which, It is . . . that,* and the like:

Moreover, [there is] one segment of the population [which] never seeks employment.
[There are] many women [who] never marry.
[There] is nothing wrong with it.
[It is] his last book [that] shows his genius best.
[It is] this [that] is important.

The bracketed words can disappear without a ripple. Furthermore, *It is* frequently misleads your reader by seeming to mean something specific (*beer,* in the following example):

> Several members voted for beer. *It is* hard to get *it* through some
> people's heads that minors can't buy it. [Some people never
> learn that minors can't buy it.]

Cut every *it* not referring to something. Next to activating your
passives, and cutting the passivistic *there is*'s and *it is*'s, perhaps
nothing so improves your prose as to go through it systematically
deleting every *to be*, every *which, that, who,* and *whom* not needed
for utter clarity or for spacing out a thought. All of your sentences
will feel better.

Beware the* of-and-which *disease. The passive sentence also
breaks out in a rash of *of*'s and *which*'s, and even the active sentence
may suffer. Diagnosis: something like sleeping sickness. *With*'s,
in's, *to*'s, and *by*'s also inflamed. Surgery imperative. Here is a
typical, and actual, case:

> Many biological journals, especially those *which* regularly pub-
> lish new scientific names, now state *in* each issue the exact date *of*
> publication *of* the preceding issue. *In* dealing *with* journals *which*
> do not follow this practice, or *with* volumes *which* are issued in-
> dividually, the biologist often needs *to* resort *to* indexes . . . *in*
> *order to* determine the actual date *of* publication *of* a particular
> name.

Note *of publication of* twice over, and the three *which*'s. The passage is a sleeping beauty. The longer you look at it the more useless little attendants you see. Note the inevitable passive voice
(*which are issued*) in spite of the author's active efforts. The *of*'s
accompany extra nouns, *publication* repeating *publish,* for instance.
Remedy: (1) eliminate *of*'s and their nouns, (2) change *which*-
clauses into participles, (3) change nouns into verbs. You can cut
more than a third of this passage without touching the sense (using 39 words instead of 63):

> Many biological journals, especially those regularly *publishing*
> new scientific names, now give the date of each preceding issue.
> With journals not *following* this practice, and with some books,
> the biologist must turn to indexes . . . *to date* a particular name.

I repeat: you can cut most *which*'s, one way or another, with no
loss of blood. Participles can modify their antecedents directly, since

they are verbal adjectives, without an intervening *which:* "a car *which was* going south" is "a car going south"; "a train *which is* moving" is "a moving train." Similarly with the adjective itself: "a song *which was* popular last year" is "a song popular last year"; "a person *who is* attractive" is "an attractive person." Beware of this whole crowd: *who are, that was, which are.*

If you need a relative clause, remember *that. Which* has almost completely displaced it in labored writing. *That* is still best for restrictive clauses, those necessary to definition: "A house that faces north is cool" (a participle would save a word: "A house facing north is cool"). *That* is tolerable; *which* is downright oppressive. *Which* should signal the nonrestrictive clause (the afterthought): "The house, which faces north, is a good buy." Here you need *which.* Even restrictive clauses must turn to *which* when complicated parallels arise. "He preaches the brotherhood of man *that* everyone affirms" elaborates like this: "He preaches the brotherhood of man *which* everyone affirms, *which* all the great philosophies support, but *for which* few can make any immediate concession." Nevertheless, if you need relatives, a *that* will often ease your sentences and save you from the *which*'s.

Verbs and their derivatives, especially present participles and gerunds, can also help to cure a string of *of*'s. Alfred North Whitehead, usually of clear mind, once produced this linked sausage: "Education is the acquisition *of* the art *of* the utilization *of* knowledge." Anything to get around the three *of*'s and the three heavy nouns would have been better: "Education is the art of learning to use knowledge." I have replaced *the acquisition of* with *learning,* and *the utilization of* with *to use.* Shun the *-tion*'s! Simply change your surplus *-tion*'s and *of*'s—along with your *which*-phrases —into verbs, or verbals (*to use, learning*). You will save words, and activate your sentences.

***Beware* the use of.** In fact, both *use,* as a noun, and *use,* as a verb, are dangerously wordy words. Since *using* is one of our most basic concepts, other words in your sentence will already contain it:

> **He uses rationalization. [He rationalizes.]**
> **He uses the device of foreshadowing. [He foreshadows.]**
> **Through [the use of] logic, he persuades.**
> **His [use of] dialogue is effective.**

The utilization of and *utilize* are only horrendous extremes of the same pestilence, to be stamped out completely.

Break the noun habit. Passive writing adores the noun, modifying nouns with nouns in pairs, and even in denser clusters—which then become official jargon. Break up these loggish jams, let the language flow, make one noun of the pair an adjective:

> *Teacher militancy* is not as marked in Pittsburgh. [*Teachers* are not so *militant* in Pittsburgh.]

Or convert one noun to a verb:

> *Teacher power* is less in evidence in Pittsburgh. [*Teachers demand* less in Pittsburgh.]

Of course, nouns have long served English as adjectives, as in "*rail*road," "railroad station," "*court* house," and "*noun* habit." But modern prose has aggravated the tendency beyond belief; and we get such monstrosities as *child sex education course,* whole strings of nothing but nouns. Professors of education, sociology, and psychology are the worst noun-stringers, the hardest for you not to copy if you take their courses. But we have all caught the habit. The nouns *level* and *quality* have produced a rash of redundancies. A meeting of "high officials" has now unfortunately become a meeting of "high-*level* officials." The "finest cloth" these days is always "finest *quality* cloth." Drop those two redundant clichés, and you will make a good start, and will sound surprisingly original. You can drop many an excess noun:

Wordy	*Direct*
advance notice	notice
long in size	long
puzzling in nature	puzzling
of an indefinite nature	indefinite
of a peculiar kind	peculiar
in order to	to
by means of	by
in relation to	with
in connection with	with
1971-model car	1971 car

Wherever possible, find the equivalent adjective:

of great importance	important
highest significance level	highest significant level
government spending	governmental spending
reaction fixation	reactional fixation
sex education	sexual education
teaching excellence	excellent teaching
encourage teaching quality	encourage good teaching

Or change the noun to its related participle:

advance placement	advanced placement
charter flight	chartered flight
uniform police	uniformed police
poison arrow	poisoned arrow

Or make the noun possessive:

reader interest	reader's interest
factory worker wage	factory worker's wage
veterans insurance	veterans' insurance

Or try a cautious *of:*

Wrong	*Right*
color lipstick	color of lipstick
teaching science	science of pedagogy
production quality	quality of production
high quality program	program of high quality
significance level	level of significance
a Marxist-type program	a Marxist program *or*
	a Marxist type of program

Of all our misused nouns, *type* has become peculiarly pestilential and trite. Advertisers talk of *detergent-type cleansers* instead of *detergents;* educators, of *apprentice-type situations* instead of *apprenticeships;* newspapermen, of *fascist-type organizations* instead of *fascistic organizations.* Don't copy your seniors; write boldly. We have become a nation of hairsplitters, afraid of saying *Czechoslovakia's Russian tanks* for fear that the reader will think they really belong to Russia. So the reporter writes *Russian-type tanks,* making an unnecessary distinction, and cluttering the page with one more *type-type* expression. We have forgotten that making the individual stand for the type is the simplest and oldest of metaphors: "Give us this day our daily bread." A twentieth-century man might have written "bread-type food."

The simple active sentence transmits the message by putting each word unmistakably in its place, a noun as a noun, an adjective as an adjective, with the verb—no stationary *is*—really carrying the mail. Recently, after a flood, a newspaper produced this apparently succinct and dramatic sentence: **Dead animals cause water pollution.** (The word *cause,* incidentally, indicates wasted words.) That noun *water* as an adjective throws the meaning off and takes twenty-five per cent more words than the essential active message: **Dead animals pollute water.** As you read your way into the sentence, it seems to say *dead animals cause water* (which is true enough), and then you must readjust your thoughts to accommodate *pollution.* The simplest change is from *water pollution* (noun-noun) to *polluted water* (adjective-noun), clarifying each word's function. But the supreme solution is to make *pollute* the verb it is, and the sentence a simply active message in which no word misspeaks itself. Here are the possibilities, in a scale from most active and clearest to most passive and wordiest, which may serve to chart your troubles if you get tangled in causes and nouns:

> **Dead animals pollute water.**
> **Dead animals cause polluted water.**
> **Dead animals cause water pollution.**
> **Dead animals are a factor in causing the pollution of water.**
> **Dead animals are a serious factor in causing the water pollution situation.**
> **Dead farm-type animals are a danger factor in causing the post-flood clearance and water pollution situation.**

So the message should now be clear. Write simple active sentences, outmaneuvering all passive eddies, all shallow *is*'s, *of*'s, *which*'s, and *that*'s, all overlappings, all rocky clusters of nouns: they take you off your course, delay your delivery, and wreck many a straight and gallant thought.

E X E R C I S E S

1. Write a dozen sentences in the passive voice, and change each to its active equivalent.

2. Pick five obese and passive sentences from your textbooks (including this one, if the author has slipped). Change them to clean active sentences, indicating the number of words saved in each.

3. Find in your textbooks two or three passages suffering from the *of*-and-*which* disease, *the-use-of* contagion, and the noun habit ("which shows the effect of age and intelligence level upon the use of the reflexes and the emergence of child behavior difficulties") and rewrite them in clear English.

4. Following the examples on pp. 49–52, recast these sentences in the active voice, clearing out all passive constructions, saving as many words as you can, and indicating the number saved:

> The particular topic chosen by the instructor for study in his section of English 2 must be approved by the Steering Committee. [Start with "The Steering Committee," and don't forget the economy of an apostrophe-*s*. I managed 16 words for 22.]
>
> Avoidance of such blunders should not be considered a virtue for which the student is to be commended, any more than he would be praised for not wiping his hands on the tablecloth or polishing his shoes with the guest towels. [Begin "We should not"; try *avoiding* for *avoidance*. I dropped *virtue* as redundant and scored 34 for 41.]
>
> The first respect in which too much variation seems to exist is in the care with which writing assignments are made. ["First, care in assigning"—8 for 21.]
>
> The remaining variations that will be mentioned are concerned not with the assignment of papers but with the marking and grading of them. ["Finally, I shall mention" —16 for 23.]
>
> The difference between restrictives and nonrestrictives can also be better approached through a study of the different contours that mark the utterance of the two kinds of element than through confusing attempts to differentiate the two by meaning. ["One can differentiate restrictives" —I managed 13 for 38.]

5. Here are six more to prune, especially of *that*'s, *which*'s, *who*'s, and *there is . . . which*'s (my figures again are merely guides; other solutions are equally good):

> *There is* a certain tendency to defend one's own position *which* will cause the opponent's argument to be ignored. [14 for 19]
>
> *It is* the other requirements *that* present obstacles, some *of*

which may prove insurmountable in the teaching of certain subjects. [13 for 20]

In the sort of literature-centered course being discussed here, *there is* usually a general understanding *that* themes will be based on the various literary works *that* are studied, the theory being *that* both the instruction in literature and *that* in writing will be made more effective by this interrelationship. [26 for 50]

The person *whom* he met was an expert *who was* able to teach the fundamentals quickly. [13 for 16]

They will take a pride *which is* wholly justifiable in being able to command a prose style *that is* lucid and supple. [13 for 22]

Methods *which are* unique to the historian *are illustrated* throughout the volume *in order to* show how history *is written* and how historians work. The historian's approach to his subject, *which* leads to the asking of provocative questions and to a new understanding of complex events, situations, and personalities *is probed*. The manner *in which* the historian reduces masses of chaotic fact—and occasional fancy—to reliable meaning, and the way *in which* he formulates explanations and tests them *is examined and clarified* for the student. *It is its* emphasis on historical method *which* distinguishes this book from other source readings in western civilization. The problems *which are examined* concern *themselves with* subjects *which are dealt with by* most courses in western civilization. [82 for 123]

6. Grammar

You HAVE now seen many of the ills of writing—the ailing thesis that weakens the whole system, the *of*-and-*which* disease, the recurring rash of wordiness. But many of your sentences may still suffer from ailments more deeply genetic. You can probably tell when a sentence feels bad, especially after your instructor has marked it up. You can, in other words, detect the symptoms, but to work an efficient cure you need also some skill in the old household remedies of grammar.

THE BASIC PARTS OF SPEECH

The parts of speech are the sentence's vital organs. Knowing the basic eight—nouns, pronouns, verbs, adjectives, adverbs, prepositions, conjunctions, and interjections—helps us control its midnight fevers.

N O U N S . These name something. A *proper noun* names a particular person, place, or thing. A *common noun* names a general class of things; a common noun naming a group as a single unit is a *collective noun*. A phrase or clause functioning as a noun is a *noun phrase* or a *noun clause*. Here are some examples:

Common: stone, tree, house, girl, artist, nation, democracy
Proper: George, Cincinnati, Texas, Europe, Declaration of Independence
Collective: committee, family, quartet, herd, navy, clergy, kind
Noun phrase: Riding the surf takes stamina.
Noun clause: What you say may depend on *how you say it.*

58

PRONOUNS. As their name indicates, pronouns stand "for nouns." The noun a pronoun represents is called its *antecedent*. Pronouns may be classified as follows:

> *Personal* (*standing for persons*): I, you, he, she, we, they; me, him, her, us, them; my, his, our, and so on.
>
> *Reflexive* (*turning the action back on the doer*): I hurt *myself*. They enjoy *themselves*.
>
> *Intensive* (*emphasizing the doer*): He *himself* said so.
>
> *Relative* (*linking subordinate clauses*): who, which, that, whose, whomever, whichever, and so on.
>
> *Interrogative* (*beginning a question*): who, which, what.
>
> *Demonstrative* (*pointing to things*): this, that, these, those, such.
>
> *Indefinite* (*standing for indefinite numbers of persons or things*): one, any, each, few, some, anyone, everyone, somebody, and so on.
>
> *Reciprocal* (*plural reflexives*): each other, one another.

VERBS. These express actions or states of being. A verb may be *transitive*, requiring an object to complete the thought, or *intransitive*, requiring no object for completeness. Some verbs can function either transitively or intransitively. *Linking verbs* link the subject to a state of being.

> *Transitive:* He *put* his feet on the chair. She *hit* the ceiling. They *sang* a sad old song.
>
> *Intransitive:* He *smiled*. She *cried*. They *sang* like birds.
>
> *Linking:* He *is* happy. She *feels* angry. This *looks* bad.

ADJECTIVES. These describe nouns or pronouns. An *adjectival phrase* or *adjectival clause* functions in a sentence as a single adjective would.

> *Adjectives:* The *green* house faces west. He was a *handsome* devil. The *old haunted* house was *empty*.
>
> *Adjectival phrase:* He had reached the end *of the book*.
>
> *Adjectival clause:* Here is the key *that unlocks the barn*.

ADVERBS. These describe verbs, adjectives, or other adverbs. An *adverbial phrase* or *adverbial clause* functions as a single adverb would.

Adverbs: Though *slightly* fat, he runs *quickly* and plays *extremely* well.

Adverbial phrase: He left *after the others.*

Adverbial clause: She lost the gloves *after she left the store.*

PREPOSITIONS. A preposition links a noun or pronoun to another word in the sentence. A preposition and its object form a *prepositional phrase.*

By late afternoon, Williams was exhausted.

He walked *to* his car and drove *from* the field.

CONJUNCTIONS. These join words, phrases, and clauses. Coordinating conjunctions—*and, but, or, yet, for*—join equals:

Mary *and* I won easily.

Near the shore *but* far from home, the bottle floated.

He was talented, *yet* he failed.

Subordinating conjunctions join minor thoughts to main ones:

Since it was late, they left.

He worked hard *because* he needed an A.

They stopped *after* they reached the spring.

INTERJECTIONS. These interrupt the usual flow of the sentence to emphasize feelings:

But, *oh*, the difference to me.

Mr. Dowd, *alas*, has ignored the evidence.

The consumer will suddenly discover that, *ouch*, his dollar is cut in half.

These are the parts: now for some problems in how they work.

AGREEMENT

Make your verb and its subject agree. Match singulars with singulars, plurals with plurals. You will have little trouble except when subject and verb are far apart, or when the number of the subject itself is doubtful. (Is *family* singular or plural? What about *none*—about *neither he nor she?*)

Sidestep the plural constructions that fall between your singular subject and its verb:

Faulty: The *attention* of the students *wander* out the window.
Revised: The *attention* of the students *wanders* out the window.

Faulty: The *plaster,* as well as the floors, *need* repair.
Revised: The *plaster,* as well as the floors, *needs* repair.

Collective nouns (*committee, jury, herd, group, family, kind, quartet*) are single units; give them singular verbs, or plural members:

Faulty: Her *family were* ready.
Revised: Her *family was* ready.

Faulty: The *jury have disagreed* among themselves.
Revised: The *jurors have disagreed* among themselves.

Faulty: These *kind* of muffins *are* delicious.
Revised: These muffins are delicious.
Revised: This kind of muffin *is* delicious.

Watch out for the indefinite pronouns—*each, neither, anyone, everyone, no one, none, everybody, nobody.* Each of these is (not *are*) singular in idea, yet each flirts with the crowd from which it singles out its idea: each of *these,* either of *them,* none of *them.* Give all of them singular verbs.

> *None* of these men *is* a failure.
> *None* of the class, even the best prepared, *wants* the test.
> Has *everybody* paid for *his* ice cream?
> *Neither* the right nor the left *supports* the issue.

Exception: when one side, or both, of the either-or contrast is plural, the verb may be plural:

> Either the players or the coach *are* bad.
> Neither the rights of man nor the needs of the commonwealth *are* relevant to the question.

Don't let a plural noun in the predicate lure you into a plural verb:

Faulty: His most faithful rooting *section are* his family and his girl.
Revised: His most faithful rooting *section is* his family and his girl.

REFERENCE OF PRONOUNS

Match your pronouns to what they stand for. Pronouns stand for (*pro*) nouns. They *refer* back to nouns already expressed (*antecedents*), or they stand for conceptions (people, things, ideas) already established or implied, as in "*None* of *them* is perfect." Pronouns must agree with the singular and plural ideas they represent.

When a relative pronoun (*who, which, that*) is the subject of a clause, it takes a singular verb if its antecedent is singular, a plural verb if its antecedent is plural:

Phil is the only *one* of our swimmers WHO *has* won three gold medals. [The antecedent is *one*, not *swimmers*.]

Phil is one of the best *swimmers* WHO *have* ever been on the team. [The antecedent is *swimmers*, not *one*.]

Pronouns may stand either as subjects or objects of the action, and their form changes accordingly.

Use subjective pronouns for subjective functions. Those pronouns in the predicate that refer back to the subject are troublesome; keep them subjective:

This is *he*.
He discovered that it was *I*.
It was *they* who signed the treaty.

Another example is that of the pronoun in *apposition* with the subject (that is, *positioned near*, and meaning the same thing as, the subject):

We students would rather talk than sleep.

After *than* and *as*, the pronoun is usually the subject of an implied verb:

She is taller than *I* [am].
You are as bright as *he* [is].
She loves you as much as *I* [love you].

But note: "She loves you as much as [she loves] *me*." Match your pronouns to what they stand for, subjects for subjects, objects for objects.

Use a subjective pronoun as subject of a noun clause. This is the trickiest of pronominal problems, because the subject of the clause also looks like the object of the main verb:

Faulty: The sergeant asked *whomever* did it to step forward.
Revised: The sergeant asked *whoever* did it to step forward.

Similarly, parenthetical remarks like *I think, he says,* and *we believe* often make pronouns seem objects when they are actually subjects:

Faulty: Ellen is the girl *whom* I think *will succeed.*
Revised: Ellen is the girl *who* I think *will succeed.*

Use objective pronouns for objective functions. Compound objects give most of the trouble. Try the pronoun by itself: "Complimented *me,*" "sent *him,*" and so forth. These are all correct:

The mayor complimented Bill and *me.*
Between *her* and *me,* an understanding grew.
They sent it to Stuart and *him.*
. . . for you and *me.*
He would not think of letting *us* girls help him.

Use a possessive pronoun before a gerund. Gerunds are *-ing* words used as nouns, so the pronouns attached to them must say what they mean.

Faulty: She disliked *him* hunting.
Revised: She disliked *his* hunting.

The object of her dislike is not *him* but *hunting.*

Keep your antecedents clear. If an antecedent is missing, ambiguous, vague, or remote, the pronoun will suffer from "faulty reference."

Missing: In Texas *they* produce a lot of oil.
Revised: Texas produces a lot of oil.
Ambiguous: Paul smashed into a girl's car *who* was visiting his sister.
Revised: Paul smashed into the car of a *girl* visiting his sister.
Vague: Because Ann had never spoken before an audience, she was afraid of *it.*

Revised: Because Ann had never spoken before an audience, she was afraid.

Remote: The castle was built in 1537. The rooms and furnishings are carefully kept up, but the entrance is now guarded by a coin-fed turnstile. *It* still belongs to the Earl.

Revised: The castle, which still belongs to the Earl, was built in 1537. The rooms and furnishings are carefully kept up, but the entrance is now guarded by a coin-fed turnstile.

Give an indefinite or general antecedent a singular pronoun.

Faulty: Modern suburban *woman* is often more interested in *their* social standing than in *their* children.

Revised: Modern suburban *woman* is often more interested in *her* social standing than in *her* children.

Faulty: *Each* of the students hoped to follow *their* teacher's footsteps.

Revised: Each of the students hoped to follow *the* teacher's footsteps.

Faulty: If the *clergy* dares to face the new philosophy, *they* should declare *themselves*.

Revised: If the *clergy* dares to face the new philosophy, the *clergy* should declare *itself*.

SLIPS OF MIND

Don't change your subject in midstream. A shifted subject reveals uncertainty; control your subject with a firm hand.

Faulty: As *I* entered the room, *voices* could be heard.

Revised: As *I* entered the room, *I* could hear voices.

Faulty: The first *problem* is political, but *there* are *questions* of economics that are almost entirely involved in the second problem.

Revised: The first *problem* is political; the second, principally economic.

Faulty: *Jim* rolled up his sleeves, the *axe* was raised, and the *sapling* came down with four powerful strokes.

Revised: Jim rolled up his sleeves, raised the axe, and cut the sapling down with four powerful strokes.

Keep person and number consistent.   Don't slip from person to person (*I* to *they*); don't fall among singulars and plurals—or you will get bad references.

Faulty: They have reached an age when *you* should know better.
Revised: They have reached an age when *they* should know better.

Faulty: A motion *picture* can improve upon a book, but *they* usually do not.
Revised: A motion *picture* can improve upon a book, but *it* usually does not.

ALIGNING THE VERBS

Choose your tense and stay with it.   Avoid awkward shifts from past to present, as in "While the executives *stayed* in the plant, the strikers *picket.*" On the other hand, holding to one tense may confuse an actual distinction in time:

Faulty: Although the government *has stated* its policy [present perfect], the people *have* still *been* confused [present perfect].
Revised: Although the government *has stated* its policy [present perfect], the people *are* still confused [present].

Therefore, establish your tense, and then step back from it clearly into the past, or ahead from it into the future, as your thought demands:

The revolutionaries met [*past*] for the last time. The moment was [*past*] finally ripe. Discontent had been [*past perfect*] smoldering throughout the country. The government had had [*past perfect*] ample time to redress a century of abuses. Now, patience had worn [*past perfect*] thin, and plans were [*past*] ready. The explosion was [*past*] to break the old mold forever. Its effects are [*present*] still clearly visible today, and doubtless will be [*future*] even after the present order will have fallen [*future perfect*] in its turn.

Use the present tense to describe literary events:

Hamlet *finds* the king praying, but he *is* unable to act; he *lets* the opportunity slip.

Avoid awkward shifts in voice.   Changing from active to passive voice is clumsy, and may accidentally shift the subject as well.

Faulty: After they *laid out* the pattern, electrical shears *were used* to cut around it.

Revised: After they *laid out* the pattern, they *cut* around it with electrical shears.

Avoid misalignments of mood:

Faulty: If he *would have known,* he would never have said that.
Revised: If he *had known,* he would never have said that.

Faulty: He moved that the club *buy* the picture, and that the secretary *shall bill* the members.

Revised: He moved that the club *buy* the picture, and that the secretary *bill* the members.

MODIFIERS MISUSED AND MISPLACED

Keep your adjectives and adverbs straight.   The adjective sometimes wrongly crowds out the adverb: "He played a *real* conservative game." And the adverb sometimes steals the adjective's place, especially when the linking verb looks transitive but isn't (*feels, looks, tastes, smells*), making the sense wrong: "He feels *badly*" (adverb) means incompetence, not misery. Similarly, certain adjectives ending in *-ly* (*lonely, lovely, leisurely*) tend to masquerade as adverbs: "She swam *lovely*," "He walked *leisurely*." The cure is in modifying your nouns with adjectives, and modifying everything else with adverbs:

He played a *really* conservative game. [adverb]
He feels *bad.* [adjective]
She swam *beautifully.* [adverb]
He walked *slowly.* [adverb]

Some words serve both as adjectives and adverbs: *early, late, near, far, only, little, right, wrong, straight, well, better, best, fast,* for example. These words are linguistic windfalls, to be squeezed for their juice:

Think *little* of *little* things.

Near is a hard case, serving as an adjective (*the near future*) and as an adverb of place (*near the barn*), and then also trying to serve for *nearly*, the adverb of degree.

> *Faulty:* We are nowhere *near* knowledgeable enough.
> *Revised:* We are not *nearly* knowledgeable enough.

> *Faulty:* It was a *near* treasonous statement.
> *Revised:* It was a *nearly* treasonous statement.

> *Faulty:* With Dodge, he has a tie of *near*-filial rapport.
> *Revised:* With Dodge, he has an *almost* filial rapport.

Slow has a long history as an adverb, but *slowly* keeps the upper hand in print. Notice that adverbs usually go after, and adjectives before:

> The *slow* freight went *slowly*.

Make your comparisons complete.   Ask yourself "Than what?"— when you find your sentences ending with a *greener* (adjective) or a *more smoothly* (adverb):

> *Faulty:* The western plains are *flatter*.
> *Revised:* The western plains are *flatter than* those east of the Mississippi.

> *Faulty:* He plays *more skillfully*.
> *Revised:* He plays *more skillfully than* most boys his age.

> *Faulty:* Jane told her more than Ellen.
> *Revised:* Jane told her more than she told Ellen.

> *Faulty:* His income is lower than a *busboy*.
> *Revised:* His income is lower than a *busboy's*.
> *Revised:* His income is lower than that of a busboy.

Don't let your modifiers squint.   Some modifiers squint in two directions at once. Place them to modify one thing only.

> *Faulty:* They agreed *when both sides ceased fire* to open negotiations.
> *Revised:* They agreed to open negotiations *when both sides ceased fire*.

Faulty: Several delegations *we know* have failed.
Revised: *We know* that several delegations have failed.

Faulty: They hoped to try *thoroughly* to understand.
Revised: They hoped to try to understand *thoroughly*.

Faulty: He resolved to dependably develop plans.
Revised: He resolved to develop dependable plans.

Don't let your modifiers or references dangle. The *-ing* words (the gerunds and participles) tend to slip loose from the sentence and dangle, referring to nothing or the wrong thing.

Faulty: Going home, the walk was slippery. [participle]
Revised: Going home, I found the walk slippery.

Faulty: When getting out of bed, his toe hit the dresser. [gerund]
Revised: When getting out of bed, he hit his toe on the dresser.

Infinitive phrases also can dangle badly:

Faulty: To think clearly, some logic is important.
Revised: To think clearly, you should learn some logic.

Any phrase or clause may dangle:

Faulty: When only a freshman, Jim's history teacher inspired him. [phrase]
Revised: When Jim was only a freshman, his history teacher inspired him.

Faulty: After he had lectured thirty years, the average student still seemed average. [clause]
Revised: After he had lectured thirty years, he found the average student still average.

FRAGMENTS AND RUN-ONS

Align your thoughts as complete sentences. As you have seen, the fragment may have superb rhetorical force: "So what." But when fragments slip in unnoticed, they reveal a failure to grasp the sentence completely. You have lost the fundamental connection between subject and verb, and the parts related to them.

Faulty: He does not spell everything out. But rather hints that something is wrong, and leaves the rest up to the reader.

Revised: He does not *spell* everything out, but rather *hints* . . . , and *leaves* . . . . [subject with compound verb, set off by commas]

Faulty: Yet here is her husband treating their son to all that she considers evil. Plus the fact that the boy is offered beer.

Revised: Yet here is her *husband* treating their son to all that she considers evil, plus the *fact* that . . . . [*husband* and *fact* are parallel nouns, both completing the idea *here is*]

Faulty: He points out that one never knows what the future will bring. Because it is actually a matter of luck.

Revised: He points out that one never knows what the future will bring, because it is actually a matter of luck. [dependent clause now properly connected]

With run-ons—two sentences shuffled together as one—the grammatical grip is even more feeble than with the fragment. Somehow the writer has never grasped the sentence as a discrete marriage of subject and verb. All kinds of parties just stumble in together:

Faulty: He went to class, he forgot his paper. [comma-splice]
Faulty: He went to class he forgot his paper. [fused sentence]
Revised: (a) He went to class. He forgot his paper.
(b) He went to class; he forgot his paper.
(c) He went to class, but he forgot his paper.
(d) When he got to class, he found that he had forgotten his paper.

Conjunctive adverbs (*however, therefore, nevertheless, moreover, furthermore,* and others) may cause trouble.

Faulty: She bought the blouse, however her heart was not in it.
Revised: (a) She bought the blouse, but her heart was not in it.
(b) She bought the blouse; however, her heart was not in it.
(c) She bought the blouse; her heart, however, was not in it.

Similarly, transitional phrases (*in fact, that is, for example*) may run your sentences together:

Faulty: He disliked discipline, that is, he really was lazy.
Revised: (a) He disliked discipline; that is, he really was lazy.
(b) He disliked discipline, that is, anything demanding.

1. Straighten out these disagreements:

None of us are perfect.
These kind of questions are sheer absurdities.
Conservatism, as well as liberalism, are summonses for change in American life as we now know it.
Neither the tweed of his jacket nor the silk of his tie impress us.
Neither the question nor the answer seem pertinent to the issue.

2. Straighten out the faulty references:

Doug is the only one of the boys who always stand straight.
We are stronger than them.
They elected Mary and I president and vice-president respectively.
Jim will vote for whomever they say is a winner.
He opened the bird's cage, and it flew away.
It was him all right.
She disliked him whistling the same old tune.
They did it for you and I.
He will give the ticket to whomever wants it.
The average girl likes their independence.
My mother insists on me buying my own clothes.

3. Straighten out the inconsistencies of tense, voice, and mood in these two cripples:

Last year we are warned of higher taxes and getting lower taxes. This year we are promised lower taxes and getting higher taxes. What next year is holding, we can only guess. But sooner or later, we are being promised and taxed into disbelief.

A third principle that industry should recognize was the need for constant appraisal by management of an employee's progress. Management would determine what a man, when he would have been hired, were expected by it to achieve; and it then judges whether it now had had him poorly assigned. He probably knows his own limitations, and jobs beyond his capacity are poorly handled by him. But it is not enough that a manager sit down periodically with a man and reviews his performance. The important thing is that the manager understands a man well enough and be articulate enough to make sure the man himself has become conscious of his need for further development. If the manager will have been sufficiently observant, he might have helped the man to an accurate evaluation of his own potential.

4. Straighten out these adjectives and adverbs:

The demonstration reached near riot proportions.
It smells awfully.
The dress fitted her perfect.
He has a reasonable good chance.
His car had a special built engine.

5. Complete and adjust these partial thoughts:

He swims more smoothly.
The pack of a paratrooper is lighter than a soldier.
The work of a student is more intense than his parents.
This is the best painting.
The moon is smaller.

6. Unsquint these modifiers:

She planned on the next day to call him.
They asked after ten days to be notified.
The party promised to completely attempt reform.
Several expeditions we know have failed.
We wanted to win enough to cry.

7. Mend these danglers:

What we need is a file of engineers broken down by their specialties.
Following the games on television, the batting average of every player was at his fingertips.
When entering the room, the lamp fell over.
To study well, a quiet room helps.
After he arrived at the dorm, his father phoned.

8. Correct the following:

He left his second novel unfinished. Perhaps because of his basic uncertainty, which he never overcame.
He entered the race for the presidency. Knowing all along that he could not win.
He seems to play a careless game. But actually knows exactly

what he is doing, and intends to put his opponent off guard.

He played to win, that is, he gave every game all he had.

His idea of democracy was incomplete he himself had slaves.

9. Cure the following grammatical ailments:

The professor, as well as the students, were glad the course was over.

They study hard at State, but you do not have to work all the time.

Holden goes to New York and learned about life.

As he looked up, a light could be seen in the window.

A citizen should support the government, but they should also be free to criticize it.

It will all come true, for you and I.

The students always elect whomever is popular.

She hated me leaving so early.

This is one of the best essays that has been submitted.

While playing the piano, the dog sat by me and howled.

The team had a near perfect record.

Run-on sentences show a failure deeper than fragments.

10. Rewrite this fractured passage:

Twins feel special (just as all people do) and the fact that once Uncle Ted and Will's father, being twins, had the same specialness as Will and Tina do—that they played in the same places and probably dreamed the same dreams. Will and Tina assumed that they would marry some day. Thus, showing how early in life one makes plans and how they change. But somehow the specialness did not keep Ted immune plays to the fact that misfortune may be closer than striking the person in the newspaper headline—who no one really knows.

7. Punctuation

Punctuation gives the silent page some of the breath of life. It marks the pauses and emphases with which a speaker points his meaning, marking off the grammatical units. Loose punctuators have forgotten what every good writer knows: that even silent reading produces an articulate murmur in our heads, that language springs from the breathing human voice, that the beauty and meaning of language depend on what the written word makes us *hear,* on the sentence's tuning of emphasis and pause. Commas and semicolons and periods do what they can to transcribe our meaningful pauses to the printed page.

THE PERIOD: SENTENCES AND FRAGMENTS

Learn what a sentence is.   Having used sentences all our lives, we all think we know what one is. But commas still appear where periods should be, and the reader blunders ahead when he should have stopped. Think of a *sentence* as a subject completed in its verb, and tacked home with a period. A *phrase* presents no problem, since it has no verb. But a *clause,* which does have subject and verb, is nevertheless incomplete when it looks to the main sentence for fulfillment:

After the ball, the sweepers come. [Phrase]
After the ball is over, the sweepers come. [Clause]

Your sentence is complete if the first part clearly looks ahead toward the period, and if the end clearly looks back toward its beginning. If you find the first part of your sentence looking back, or looking ahead in vain, you have no sentence; you have a fragment that should be hooked, with a comma, where it belongs:

73

He dropped his teeth. *Which had cost two hundred dollars.*

A good example is Hawthorne. *A writer who can dramatize abstract moral theories.*

Cleopatra is the stronger. *Trying to create Antony in her own Egyptian image.*

The accidental fragment is almost invariably found *after* the sentence to which it belongs.

But try an occasional rhetorical fragment. Nothing so firmly demonstrates your command over the sentence as a judicious fragment, as I have already suggested (p. 42). Make it stand alone, and no mistake. Firmly. Fragments are safest and most effective, with all their transitional force, at the head of a paragraph. Such fragments are especially dramatic, economical, and close to speech:

First, a word to the wise.
Another point.
Of course.
Not at all.
Expert within limits, that is.

Notice that all these fragments—condensations, afterthoughts, answers, quiet exclamations—usually omit some hypothetical form of *is*, with its subject:

First, [here is] a word to the wise.
Of course [it is *or* he did].
[It is] not at all [so].

This kind of dramatic fragment, in other words, is talking about existences, about what *is*, letting the words assert their own being. It is exactly the kind of streamlining the Latin writers liked, and it is still swift and racy. But be careful.

THE COMMA

Learn the rules. You need only four. Put a comma:

I. Before *and, but, for, or, nor, yet, still,* when joining independent clauses.

II. Between all terms in a series, *including the last two.*

III. To set off parenthetical openers and afterthoughts.

IV. Before and after parenthetical insertions (use a *pair* of commas).

RULE I. *Put a comma before conjunctions such as* and, but, *and* for, *when joining independent clauses.*

You will be told that you may omit the comma when your two clauses are short: "He hunted and she fished." You certainly can get away with it, and in the best of publications. But it is really the first tiny slip toward utter abandon. Your clauses will grow longer. You will begin to touch in a comma only now and then, still leaving the main gap between clauses unplugged. You will omit commas before *but* and *for* and really throw your reader off. Nothing is wrong with "He hunted, and she fished." With the comma, in fact, it shows the slight pause you make when you say it. Stick to the rule, and you can't go wrong. And you will greatly improve your sense of style.

Think of the **,and** as a unit equivalent to the period. The period, the semicolon, and the **,and** all separate independent clauses, but with different emphases:

. He was tired. He went home.

; He was tired; he went home.

,and He was tired, and he went home.

If you can only think of the **,and** or the **,but** as a unit, perfectly equivalent to the period, and the semicolon as a buffer between independent clauses, you will have mastered the basic problem in punctuation, the cause of most trouble.

What you need is a firm rule to follow, one to break only in airier moments, with a full sense of release and a clear gain in meaning. Look again at White's *when* sentence:

Next morning when the first light came into the sky and the sparrows stirred in the trees, when the cows rattled their chains and the rooster crowed and the early automobiles went whispering along the road, Wilbur awoke . . . .

White omits several commas before *and*, but the reason is dazzlingly clear: he is regimenting short coordinate clauses under one subordinator, and a comma after *sky*, for instance, would block the *when* from the *sparrows* and throw the clauses out of rank. For reasons of rank, he also omits the "introductory" comma after *Next morning*. A comma here, since there are only two commas controlling the whole long sentence, would have made *Next morning* too prominent, making it seem equal to the long *when* elements.

Your punctuation, or lack of it, signals your meaning as it comes in, word by word. The **,and** tells your reader that a whole new predication is coming; just plain **and** tells him to expect only a smaller unit:

He hunted the hills and . . . .

brings an entirely different expectation from:

He hunted the hills, and . . . .

In the first, you expect something like *dales,* something parallel to *hills.* In the second, you expect another subject and predicate: "and he found . . . ," or "and they were . . . ."

Omitting the comma between independent clauses joined by *and* really makes a false parallel, and the silence of print has often encouraged our error. When you *say* "hills and dales," you do not pause. When you *say* ". . . hills, and he found . . . ," you do pause. English invariably expresses this difference in meaning by pausing or not. Modern linguists, who call this pause a "double-bar juncture," have reminded us that commas represent meaning.

The same may be seen with *but, or,* and *yet:*

She was naughty but nice.
She was naughty, but that is not our business.

Wear your jacket or coat.
Wear your jacket, or you will catch cold.

It was strong yet sweet.
It was strong, yet it was not unpleasant.

Of course, you may use a comma in *all* the examples above, if your sense demands it, because the contrast set by *but, or,* and *yet* often urges a comma, whether or not full predication follows: "It was strong, yet sweet." You will notice that you always pause where the commas are.

You need a comma before *for* and *still* even more urgently. Without it, their conjunctive meaning changes; they assume their ordinary roles, *for* as a preposition, *still* as an adjective or adverb:

She liked him still . . . . [that is, either *yet* or *quiet!*]
She liked him, still she could not marry him.

She liked him for his money.
She liked him, for a good man is hard to find.

An observation: *for* is the weakest of all the coordinators—almost a subordinator, perilously close to *because*. *For* can seem moronic, if cause and effect are fairly obvious: "She liked him, for he was kind." Either make a point of the cause by full subordination—"She liked him *because* he was kind"—or flatter the reader with a semicolon: "She liked him; he was kind." *For* is effective only when the cause is somewhat hard to find: "Blessed are the meek, for they shall inherit the earth."

RULE II. *Put commas between all terms in a series, including the last two.*

words, phrases, or clauses in a series
to hunt, to fish, and to hike
He went home, he went upstairs, and he could remember nothing.
He liked oysters, soup, roast beef, wine, and women.

The linguists' recordings will show a pause between the last two items of a series as well as between any two: not *wine-and-women*, but *wine*, and *women*. The good punctuator would drop the last comma only if he meant *wine and women* as a unit equivalent to *oysters*. Since the last element will always have some climactic or anticlimactic effect, solemn or humorous, don't blur it into the one preceding. Keep *wine* and *women* separate.

By carefully separating all elements in a series, you keep alive a final distinction long since lost in the daily press, the one Mrs. Woolf makes (see p. 42): "urbane, polished, brilliant, imploring and commanding him . . . ." *Imploring and commanding* is syntactically equal to each one of the other modifiers in the series. If Mrs. Woolf customarily omitted the last comma, as she does not, she could not have reached for that double apposition. The muscle would have been dead. These other examples of double apposition can give you an idea of its effectiveness:

They cut out his idea, root and branch.
He lost all his holdings, houses and lands.
He loved to tramp the woods, to fish and to hunt.

A comma makes a great deal of difference, of sense and distinction.
Notice the difference between the following adjectives in series:

a good, unexpected, natural rhyme
a good old battered hat

With adjectives in series only your sense can guide you. If each seems to modify the noun directly, as in the first example above, use commas. If each seems to modify the total accumulation of noun and adjectives, as with *good* and *old* in the second phrase, do not use commas. Say your phrases aloud, and put your commas in the pauses that distinguish your meaning.

Finally, a special case. You can sometimes join clauses with commas, omitting the conjunctions:

She sighed, she cried, she almost died.
I couldn't do it, I tried, I let them all get away.
It passed, it triumphed, it was a good bill.
I came, I saw, I conquered.

The rhetorical intensity of this construction—the Greeks called it *asyndeton*—is obvious. The language is breathless, or grandly emphatic. As Aristotle once said, it is a person trying to say many things at once. The subjects repeat themselves, the verbs overlap, the idea accumulates a climax. By some psychological magic, the clauses of this construction usually come in three's. The comma is its sign. But unless you have a stylistic reason for such a flurry of clauses, go back to the normal conjunction, semicolon, or period.

RULE III. *Set off parenthetical openers and after-thoughts with a comma.*

Again, note the preliminary pause that expresses your meaning:

Besides, she hated it.
However, she liked him.
Inside, everything was snug.
For several reasons, they stayed home.
Being of stout heart, he dieted.
A good man at poker, he still failed at bridge.
Although several looked bored, he kept on talking.
Because it never gets cold, they wear few clothes.
If it is not too much trouble, punctuate accurately.

First observation: A comma often makes all the difference:

However she tried, she could not do it.
However, she tried.
However she tried. [??]

You can usually avoid the danger of forgetting the comma and spoiling the sense by substituting *but* for your initial *however's*. Put your *however's* (as conjunctive adverbs) within the sentence between commas: "She tried, however, a little longer."

With afterthoughts, the rule still holds: ordinarily you should set them off with a comma. But close sequences of cause and effect (even in openers) often make the comma optional with *for, because,* and *if,* and occasionally with others.

> They stayed home for several reasons.
> For several reasons they stayed home.
> Everything was snug inside.
> They wear few clothes because it never gets cold.
> Punctuate accurately if you can.

Emphasis makes the difference. A comma would have damaged none of them (when in doubt, follow the rule); it would merely have changed their rhetoric.

R U L E   I V . *Enclose parenthetical insertions with a pair of commas.*

You are cutting the sentence in two, and inserting something necessary. If you do not tie off both ends, your thought will die on the table:

> When he packs his bag, however he goes.
> The car, an ancient Packard is still running.
> April 10, 1980 is agreeable as a date for final payment.
> That handsome man in the ascot tie, is the groom.
> John Jones, Jr. is wrong.

You do not mean that 1980 is agreeable, nor that Junior is wrong. All parenthetical insertions need a *pair* of commas:

> The case, *nevertheless,* was closed.
> She will see, *if she has any sense at all,* that he is right.

The same rule applies, of course, to *nonrestrictive* remarks, phrases, and clauses—all elements that are simply additive, explanatory, and hence parenthetical:

> John, *my friend,* will do what he can.
> The taxes, *which are reasonable,* will be paid.
> Andy, *his project sunk, his hopes shattered,* was speechless.
> That man, *who knows,* is not talking.

Think of *nonrestrictive* as "nonessential" to your meaning, hence set off by commas. Think of *restrictive* as essential and "restricting" your meaning, hence not set off at all (use *which* for nonrestrictives, *that* for restrictives; see p. 52):

> The taxes that are reasonable will be paid.
> Southpaws who are superstitious will not pitch on Friday nights.
> The man who knows is not talking.

Commas are often optional. The difference between a restrictive and a nonrestrictive meaning may be very slight. For example, you may take our recent bridegroom either way (but not halfway):

> That handsome man, in the ascot tie, is the groom. [nonrestrictive]
> That handsome man in the ascot tie is the groom. [restrictive]

Your meaning will dictate your choice. But use *pairs* of commas or none at all. Never separate subject and verb, or verb and object, with just one comma.

Some finer points. One comma of a pair enclosing an inserted remark may coincide with, and, in a sense, overlay, a comma "already there":

> In each box, a bottle was broken.
> In each box, however, a bottle was broken.

> The team lost, and the school was sick.
> The team lost, in spite of all, and the school was sick.

> The program will work, but the cost is high.
> The program will work, of course, but the cost is high.

Between the coordinate clauses, however, a semicolon would be clearer:

> The team lost, in spite of all; and the school was sick.

Beware: *however,* between commas, cannot substitute for *but.* You will be using a comma where a full stop (period or semicolon) should be.

> *Wrong:*
> He wore a hat, however, it looked terrible.
> *Right (notice the two meanings):*
> He wore a hat; however, it looked terrible.
> He wore a hat, however; it looked terrible.

But a simple, *but* avoids both the ambiguity of the floating *however* and the ponderosity of anchoring it with a semicolon, fore and aft: "He wore a hat, but it looked terrible."

Another point. *But* may absorb the first comma of a pair enclosing an introductory remark (although it need not do so):

At any rate, he went.
But, at any rate, he went.
But at any rate, he went.
But [,] if we want another party, we had better clean up.
The party was a success, but [,] if we want another one, we had
    better clean up.

And of course you should put the comma *inside* ALL quotation marks:

"He is a nut," she said.
She called him a "nut," and walked away.

SEMICOLON AND COLON

Use the semicolon only where you could also use a period, unless desperate. Confusion comes from the belief that the semicolon is either a weak colon or a strong comma. It is most effective as neither. It is best as a kind of light period, a separator of contrasts. *Never* use it as a colon: its effect is exactly opposite. A colon, as in the preceding sentence, is a green light; a semicolon, as in this sentence, is a stop sign.

Of course, you may occasionally need to unscramble a long line of phrases and clauses:

You should see that the thought is full, the words well cleaned,
    the points adjusted; and then your sentence will be ready to go.
    (*Note that the period rule would still guide you here:* ". . . ad-
    justed. And then . . . .")
Composition is hard because we often must discover our ideas by
    writing them out, clarifying them on paper; because we must
    find a clear and reasonable order for ideas the mind presents
    simultaneously; and because we must find, by trial and error,
    exactly the right words to convey our ideas and our feelings
    about them.

But the semicolon is better when it pulls related sentences together:

> She liked him; he was good to her; he had money in the bank.

And better still when it pivots a contrast:

> Work when you work; play when you play.
> The semicolon is a stop sign; the colon, a green light.

Notice that the semicolon (like the colon) goes *outside* quotation marks:

> This was no "stitch in time"; it was complete reconstruction.

PARENTHESIS AND DASH

The dash says aloud what the parenthesis whispers. Both enclose interruptions too big for a pair of commas to hold. The dash is the more useful—since whispering tends to annoy—and will remain useful only if not overused. Overdone, it can be a sign of ignorance, or of laziness. But a well-cultivated dash will give you the ultimate in urbane control. It can serve as a conversational colon. It can set off a concluding phrase—for emphasis. It can bring long introductory matters to focus, as in Freud's sentence on page 41. It can insert a full sentence—a clause is really an incorporated sentence—directly next to a key word. It allows a structural complexity with all the tone and alacrity of talk.

When one of a pair of dashes falls where a comma would be, it absorbs the comma:

> If one wanted to go, he certainly could.
> If one wanted to go—whether he was invited or not—he certainly could.

Not so with the semicolon:

> He wanted to go—whether he was invited or not; she had more sense.

To indicate the dash, type two hyphens (--) flush against the words they separate—not one hyphen between two spaces, nor a hyphen looking exactly like a hyphen.

Put commas and periods *outside* a parenthetical group of words (like this one). (But if you make an entire sentence parenthetical, put the period inside.)

BRACKETS

Brackets indicate your own words inserted or substituted within a quotation from someone else: "Byron had already suggested that [they] had killed John Keats." You have substituted "they" for "the gentleman of *The Quarterly Review*" to suit your own context; you do the same when you interpolate a word of explanation. *Do not use parentheses:* they mark the enclosed words as part of the original quotation. Don't claim innocence because your typewriter lacks brackets. Just leave spaces and draw them in later, or type slant lines and tip them with pencil or with the underliner on your "6" key:

$$\mathcal{L} \cdot \cdot \cdot \mathcal{J}$$

QUOTATION MARKS

Put quotation marks around quotations that "run directly into your text" (like this), but *not* around quotations set off from the text and indented. Periods and commas go *inside* quotation marks; semicolons and colons go *outside*.

This was no "stitch in time"; it was complete reconstruction.
This was another "thorn in the side."
He thought that "seeing is believing," until today.
In Greece, it was "know thyself"; in America, it is "know thy neighbor."
He left after "Hail to the Chief": he could do nothing more.

Although logic seems to demand the period or comma outside the quotation marks, convention has put them inside for the sake of appearance, even when the sentence ends in a single quoted word or letter:

Clara Bow was said to have "It."
Mark it with "T."

If you have seen the periods and commas outside, you were reading a British book or a freshman paper.

If you quote a phrase already containing quotation marks, reduce the original double marks (") to single ones ('):

Original	*Your quotation*
The word "cue" is interesting.	He writes that the "word 'cue' is interesting."

Notice what happens when the quotation within your quotation falls at the end:

Original	*Your quotation*
The Japanese call albatross "aho dori."	Jones reports that the "Japanese call albatross 'aho dori.' "

ELLIPSIS

(1) Use three spaced periods . . . (the ellipsis mark) when omitting something from a quotation. Do *not* use them in your own text in place of a dash, or in mere insouciance. (2) If you omit the end of a sentence, add the period . . . ✓(3) If your omission falls after a completed sentence, add the ellipsis mark to the period already there.✓. . . I have put a check over the periods. Notice the difference in spacing. Note that each placement of the ellipsis mark means something different.

Here is an uncut passage, followed by a shortened version showing in succession the three kinds of ellipsis:

> To learn a language, learn as thoroughly as possible a few everyday sentences. This will educate your ear for all future pronunciations. It will give you a fundamental grasp of structure. Some of the details of grammar will begin to appear. It will give you confidence. If you go abroad, you can buy a newspaper and find your way back to the hotel.
>
> (1)
> To learn a language, learn . . . a few everyday sentences. This (2)
> will educate your ear . . . . It will give you a fundamental grasp (3)   (3)
> of structure. . . . It will give you confidence. . . . you can buy a newspaper and find your way back to the hotel.

APOSTROPHE

Add 's to form the singular possessive, even with words already ending in *s* (*dog's life, Yeats's poems, Marx's ideas, Charles's crown, Leavis's error*). A few plurals also form the possessive by adding 's (*children's hour, men's room, women's pool, mice's holiday, sheep's bellwether*). But most plurals take the apostrophe after the *s* (*witches' sabbath, the Browns' house, citizens' rights*).

Some people merely add the apostrophe after words ending in *s*: *boss' daughter, Williams' edict, Sis' plans*. But we say *boss's daughter* ("bossuz daughter") and *Sis's plans*, and we should write, and say, *Williams's edict, Dickens's novels*, and *Adams's horse* to distinguish Williams from William, Dickens from Dicken, and Adams from Adam.

The apostrophe can clarify clusters of nouns: *Alistair Jones Combo* is *Alistair Jones's Combo*; the *church barbecue chicken sale* is the *church's barbecued chicken sale; student protest* is *students' protest*. Distinguish your modifiers, and keep your possessions.

E X E R C I S E S

1. Write five fragments that are unmistakable accidents, crying out for attachment to some governing sentence. Then write five complete sentences with these fragments properly attached.

2. Write three groups of three or four sentences, each group containing a rhetorical fragment that cannot be mistaken for a mistake.

3. Write a dozen pairs of sentences, using the six conjunctions *and, but, for, or, yet, still*, on the pattern:

> **He hunted the hills and . . . .**
> **He hunted the hills, and . . . .**

4. Run off five or six sentences with concluding double appositives which might look like parts of a simple series but which are not: "He loved to camp, to hunt and to fish."

5. Write four or five asyndetic sentences (see p. 78), each with three clauses.

6. Master *however* by writing five or six groups of three sentences on the following pattern:

> **However she tried, she could not do it.**
> **She tried, however, a very long time.**
> **She tried; however, she could not do it.**

7. Write five or six pairs of sentences to practice enclosing parenthetical insertions within a pair of commas:

April 10 is fine.
April 10, 1990, is fine.
The taxes will be paid.
The taxes, which are reasonable, will be paid.

8. Do the same with dashes and with parentheses.

9. Write six pairs of sentences showing the difference between non-restrictive and restrictive clauses, on the pattern:

The taxes, which are reasonable, will be paid.
The taxes that are reasonable will be paid.

10. Write six compound sentences, using a semicolon between two contrasting independent clauses.

8. Words

ERE is the word. Sesquipedalian or short, magniloquent or low, Latin or Anglo-Saxon, Celtic, Danish, French, Spanish, Indian, Hindustani, Dutch, Italian, Portuguese, Chinese, Hebrew, Turkish, Greek—a million words at our disposal, if we are disposed to use them. Although no language is richer than English, our expository vocabularies average probably fewer than 8,000 words. We could all increase our active vocabularies; we all have a way to go to possess our inheritance.

VOCABULARY

If you can increase your hoard, you increase your chances of finding the right word, *le mot juste*, when you need it. Read as widely as you can, and look words up the second or third time you meet them. I once knew a man who swore he learned three new words a day from his reading by using each at least once in conversation. I didn't ask him about *polyphiloprogenitive* or *antidisestablishmentarianism*. It depends a little on the crowd. But the idea is sound. The bigger the vocabulary the more various the ideas one can get across with it—the more the shades and intensities of meaning.

The big vocabulary also needs the little word. The vocabularian often strands himself on a Roman cloud and forgets the Anglo-Saxon ground—the common ground between him and his audience. So do not forget the little things, the *stuff, lint, get, twig, snap, go, mud, coax*. Hundreds of small words not in immediate vogue can refresh your vocabulary. The Norse and Anglo-Saxon adjectives ending in *-y* (*muggy, scrawny, drowsy*), for instance, rarely appear

87

in sober print. The minute the beginner tries to sound dignified, in comes a misty layer of words a few feet off the ground and nowhere near heaven, the same two dozen or so, most of them verbs. One or two will do no harm, but any accumulation is fatal—words like *depart* instead of *go:*

accompany—go with	place—put
appeared—looked *or* seemed	possess—have
arrive—come	prepare—get ready
attempt—try	questioned—asked
become—get	receive—get
cause—make	relate—tell
cease—stop	remain—stay
complete—finish	remove—take off
continue—keep on	retire—go to bed
delve—dig	return—go back
discover—find	secure—get
locate—find	transform—turn

I add one treasured noun: *manner—way.* The question, as always, is one of meaning. *Manner* is something with a flourish; *way* is the usual way. But the beginner makes no distinctions, losing the normal *way,* and meaning, in a false flourish of *manners.* Similarly, "She *placed* her cigarettes on the table" is usually not what the writer means. *Delve* is something that happens only when students begin to meditate. *Get* and *got* may be too colloquial for regular writing, but a discreet one or two can limber many a stiff sentence. Therefore, fit the elegant Latin to the commonplace Anglo-Saxon. But shun the frayed gentility of *secure* and *place* and *remain,* whose shades of meaning you can find in your dictionary.

Abraham Lincoln read the dictionary from cover to cover, and you really can browse it with pleasure, looking at the pictures and finding out about aardvarks and axolotyles, jerboas and jerkins. You can amaze yourself at the number of things *set* can mean. Best of all, you can look at a word's derivation and get a quick sense of our linguistic history, of families of words and ideas, of how some meanings have changed and some have persisted through centuries and across continents. *Mid,* for instance, is still what it has been for the last 5,000 years, persisting in most of the Indo-European languages all the way from Old Norse to Sanskrit, and giving English a whole family of words from *middle* to *intermezzo.* Acquaintance with a family can make you feel at home. You can know and use a *ramp*, or a *rampage*, or a lion *rampant* familiarly, once you see the Old French for *climb* in all three. You can cut your meaning close to the old root, as in "He was *enduring* and *hard* as nails," where the Latin *durus* ("hard") has suggested its Anglo-Saxon synonym and given you a phrase your readers will like, though most of them won't know why.

Through the centuries, English has added Latin derivatives alongside the Anglo-Saxon words already there, keeping the old with the new: after the Anglo-Saxon *deor* (*deer*) came the *beast* and then the *brute*, both from Latin through French, and the *animal* straight from Rome. Although we use more Anglo-Saxon in assembling our sentences (*to, by, with, though, is*), well over half our total vocabulary comes one way or another from Latin. The things of this world tend to be Anglo-Saxon (*man, house, stone, wind, rain*); the abstract qualities, Latin and French (*value, duty, contemplation*).

Our big words are Latin and Greek. Your reading acquaints you with them; your dictionary will show you their prefixes and roots. Learn the common prefixes and roots (see Exercises, this section), and you can handle all kinds of foreigners at first encounter: *con-cession* (going along with), *ex-clude* (lock out), *pre-fer* (carry before), *sub-version* (turning under), *trans-late* (carry across), *claus-tro-phobia* (dread of being locked in), *hydro-phobia* (dread of water), *ailuro-philia* (love of cats), *megalo-cephalic* (big-headed), *micro-meter* (little-measurer). You can even, for fun, coin a word to suit the occasion: *megalopede* (big-footed). You can remember that *intra-mural* means "within the (college) walls," and that "intermural sports," which is the frequent mispronunciation and misspelling, would mean something like "wall battling wall," a physical absurdity.

Besides a good dictionary, you should own Roget's *Thesaurus*, the treasury of synonyms ("together-names"), in which you can find the word you couldn't think of, and all the shades of good and bad you want, from *pants* through *trousers* to *galligaskins*. Peter Roget's great work of 1852, compiled for fifty years and since augmented and refined, is indeed a treasury. Any one word will open the door. And once the writer sees all the resources, all the related words, "an instinctive tact," as Roget says, "will rarely fail to lead him to the proper choice." Checking for meaning in a dictionary will assure that your instincts are sound.

ABSTRACT AND CONCRETE

Every good stylist has perceived, in one way or another, the distinction between abstract and concrete words. Tangible things—things we can touch—are "concrete"; their qualities, along with all our emotional, intellectual, and spiritual states, are "abstract." The rule for a good style is to be as concrete as you can, to illustrate tangibly your general propositions, to use *shoes* and *ships* and *sealing wax* instead of *commercial concomitants*. But this requires constant effort: our minds so crave abstraction that we can hardly pin them down to specifics.

Abstraction, a "drawing out from," is the very nature of thought. Thought moves from concrete to abstract. In fact, *all* words are abstractions. *Stick* is a generalization of all sticks, the crooked and the straight, the long and the short, the peeled and the shaggy. No word fits its object like a glove, because words are not things: words represent our *ideas* of things. They are the means by which we class eggs and tents and trees so that we can handle them as ideas —not as actual things but as *kinds* of things. A man can hold an egg in his hand, but he cannot think about it, or talk about it, unless he has some larger idea with which his mind, too, can grasp it, some idea like *thing*, or *throwing thing*, or *egg*—which classes this one white spheroid with all the eggs he has known, from ostrich to hummingbird, with the *idea* of egg. One word per item would be useless; it would be no idea at all, since ideas represent not items, but *classes* of items.

So before we disparage abstraction, we should understand that it is an essential distillation, a primary and natural and continual mental process. We cannot do without it. We could not make four of two and two. So we make abstractions of abstractions to handle bigger and bigger groups of ideas. *Egg* becomes *food*, and *food* becomes *nourishment*. We also classify all the psychic and physical qualities we can recognize: *candor, truth, anger, beauty, negligence, temperament*. But because our thoughts drift upward, we need always to look for the word that will bring them nearer earth, that will make our abstractions seem visible and tangible, that will make them graspable. We have to pull them down within reach of our reader's own busily abstracting headpiece.

We must pin our abstractions down with constant comparisons to the concrete eggs from which they sprang. I might have written that sentence—as I found myself starting to do: "Abstractions should be actualized by a process of constant comparisons with the concrete objects which they represent." But note what I have done to pull this down within reach. First, I have used *we;* that is, you and me, real people. I have cut the inhuman passive voice to put us in the act. Then I have changed *actualize* to *pin down*, a visible action that, being commonplace and proverbial, makes us feel at home among the abstractions. I have replaced the abstract *by a process of* with its simpler abstract equivalent *with*. More important, I have made *eggs* stand for all objects—and note how easily our abstracters take this in. Furthermore, I have punned on *concrete,* making it, for a fleeting instant, into cement. How? By choosing *egg,* something that could really be made out of concrete, instead of *stick* (which I had first put there): a concrete stick is not much as a physical possibility. Finally, I have gone on to use *egg* also as a real egg by having the abstract ideas spring from it. Later, I almost changed *sprang* to *hatched,* but decided that this was too vivid. It would make the concrete egg too nearly real, and the picture of broken cement with fluffy abstractions peeping forth would have gotten in the way of the idea—that is, the disembodied abstract concept—I was trying to convey.

METAPHOR

As you have probably noticed, I have been using metaphors— the most useful way of making our abstractions concrete. The word is Greek for "transfer" (*meta* equals *trans* equals *across; phor* equals *fer* equals *ferry*). The idea is that of representing something as if it were something else, objects as if all of them were eggs, abstractions as if they were chickens that are also vaguely like flowers springing, thought as if it were rising steam. Metaphors illustrate, in a word, our general ideas. I might have written at length about how an idea is like an egg. I did, in fact, follow each declaration with an example, and I illustrated the point with a man holding an egg. But the metaphor makes the comparison at a stroke. I used our common word *grasp* for "understanding," comparing the mind to something with hands, *transferring* the physical picture of the clutching hand to the invisible mental act.

Almost all our words are metaphors, usually with the physical picture faded. *Transfer* itself pictures a physical portage. When the company *transfers* its men, it is sending them about the country as if by piggyback, or raft, or whatever. But mercifully the physical facts have faded—*transfer* has become a "dead metaphor"—and we can use the word in comfortable abstraction. Now, precisely because we are constantly abstracting, constantly letting the picture fade, you can use metaphor to great advantage—or disastrously, if your eyes aren't sharp. With metaphors you avoid the nonpictorial quality of most of our writing; you make your writing both vivid and unique. As Aristotle said, the metaphor is clear, agreeable, and strange; like a solved riddle, it is the most delightful of teachers.

Metaphor works at about four levels, each with a different clarity and force (and, as you will see, we must here distinguish between the general idea of "metaphor" as the whole process of transfer, and that specific thing called "a metaphor"):

> *Simile:* She was *like* a horse.
> She stopped *as* a horse stops.
> She stopped *as if* she were a horse.
> *Metaphor:* She was a horse.
> *Implied metaphor:* She snorted and tossed her mane.
> *Dead metaphor:* She bridled.

The simile is the most obvious of the metaphors, and hence would seem elementary. But it has powers of its own, particularly in its *as if* variation, where the writer seems to be trying urgently to express the inexpressible, comparing his subject to several different possibilities, no one wholly adequate. The simile has a high poetic energy. D. H. Lawrence uses it frequently, as in the following paragraph (with my italics) from *The Plumed Serpent:*

> The lake was quite black, *like a great pit.* The wind suddenly blew with violence, with a strange ripping sound in the mango trees, *as if some membrane in the air were being ripped.* The white-flowered oleanders in the garden below leaned over quite flat, their white flowers ghostly, going right down to the earth, in the pale beam of the lamp—*like a street lamp*—that shone on the wall at the front entrance.

The plain metaphor makes the comparison in one imaginative leap. It is shorthand for "as if she were a horse"; it pretends, by exaggeration (*hyperbole*), that she *is* a horse. The effect is sometimes humorous or bitter, but can be simply and aptly visual: "The road was a ribbon of silver."

The implied metaphor is the most widely useful. It operates

most often among the verbs, as in *snorted* and *tossed,* the horsy verbs suggesting "horse." Most ideas can suggest analogues of physical processes or natural history. Give your television system *tentacles,* and you have compared TV to an octopus, with all its lethal and wiry suggestions. You can have your school spirit *fall below zero.* You can even pun on the physical Latin components in our abstract words, turning them back into their original suggestions of physical acts, as in "The *enterprise* grabbed everything" (some beast or army is rushing in), for *enterprise* means in Latin something like "to rush in and grab." Too subtle? No, the contrast between *enterprise* and *grabbed* will please anyone, and the few who see it all will be delighted.

Enterprise is really a dead metaphor, and the art of resuscitation is the metaphorist's finest skill. It comes from liking words, and paying attention to what they say. The punster makes the writer, if he can restrain himself. Simply add onto the dead metaphor enough implied metaphors to get the circulation going again: *She bridled, snorting and tossing her mane. She bridled* means, by itself, as we have abstracted it, nothing more than "reacted disdainfully." By bringing the metaphor back to life, we keep the general meaning but also restore the physical picture of a horse lifting its head and arching its neck against the bridle. It is exhilarating. We recognize *bridle* concretely and truly for the first time. We know the word, and we know the woman. We have an image of her, a posture vaguely suggestive of a horse.

Perhaps the best dead metaphors to revive are those in proverbial clichés. See what Thoreau does (in his journal) with *spur of the moment:*

> I feel the spur of the moment thrust deep into my side. The present is an inexorable rider.

Or again, when in *Walden* he speaks of wanting "to improve the nick of time, and notch it on my stick too," and of not being *thrown off the track* "by every nutshell and mosquito's wing that falls on the rails." In each case, he takes the proverbial phrase literally and physically, adding an attribute or two to bring the old metaphor back alive.

You can go too far, of course. The metaphors can be too thick and vivid, and the obvious pun brings a howl of protest. Jane Austen disliked metaphors, as Mary Lascelles notes (*Jane Austen and Her Art,* pp. 111–12), and reserved them for her hollow characters. I myself have advised scholars not to use them because they are so often overworked and so often tangled in physical impossibilities. "The violent population explosion has paved the way for new intellectual growth" looks pretty good—until you realize that explosions do not pave, and that new vegetation does not grow up through pavement. The metaphor, then, is your most potent device. It makes your thoughts concrete, and your writing vivid. It tells in an instant how your subject looks to you. But it is dangerous. It should be quiet, almost unnoticed, with all details agreeing and all absolutely consistent with the natural universe.

ALLUSION

Allusions also illustrate your general idea by referring it to something else, making it take your reader as Grant took Richmond, making you the Mickey Mantle of the essay, or the Mickey Mouse. Allusions depend on common knowledge. Like the metaphor, they illustrate the remote with the familiar—a familiar place, or event, or personage. "He looked . . . like a Japanese Humphrey Bogart," writes William Bitner of French author Albert Camus, and we instantly see a face like the one we know so well. Perhaps the most effective allusions depend on a knowledge of literature. When Thoreau writes that "the winter of man's discontent was thawing as well as the earth," we get a secret pleasure from recognizing this as an allusive borrowing from the opening lines of Shakespeare's *Richard III:* "Now is the winter of our discontent/ Made glorious summer by this sun of York." Thoreau flatters us by assuming we are as well read as he. We do not need to catch the allusion to enjoy his point, but if we catch it, we do feel a sudden fellowship of knowledge with him. We now see the full metaphorical force, Thoreau's and Shakespeare's both, heightened as it is by our remembrance of Richard Crookback's twisted discontent, an allusive illustration of all our pitiful resentments now thawing with the spring.

DICTION

"What we need is a mixed diction," said Aristotle, and his point remains true twenty-three centuries and several languages later. The aim of style, he says, is to be clear but distinguished. For clarity, we need common, current words; but used alone, these are commonplace, and as ephemeral as everyday talk. For distinction, we need words not heard every minute, unusual words, strange words, foreign words, metaphors; but used alone, these become gibberish. What we need is a diction that marries the popular with the dignified, the clear current with the sedgy margins of language and thought.

Not too low, not too high; not too simple, not too hard—an easy breadth of idea and vocabulary. English is peculiarly well endowed for this Aristotelian mixture. The long abstract Latin words and the short concrete Anglo-Saxon ones give you all the range you need. For most of your ideas you can find Latin and Anglo-Saxon partners. In fact, for many ideas you can find a whole spectrum of synonyms from Latin through French to Anglo-Saxon, from general to specific: from *intrepidity* to *fortitude* to *valor* to *courage* to *bravery* to *pluck* to *guts*. You can choose the high word for high effect, or you can get tough with Anglo-Saxon specifics. But you do not want all Anglo-Saxon, and you must especially guard against sobriety's luring you into all Latin. Tune your diction agreeably between the two extremes.

The mixing of Latin and Anglo-Saxon, as John Crowe Ransom has noted, is what gives Shakespeare much of his power:

> **This my hand will rather**
> **The multitudinous seas incarnadine,**
> **Making the green one red.**

The short Anglo-Saxon *seas* works sharply between the two magnificent Latin words, as do the three short Anglo-Saxons that bring the big passage to rest, contrasting the Anglo-Saxon *red* with its big Latin synonym, *incarnadine*. William Faulkner, who has soaked himself in Shakespeare, gets much the same power from the same mixture. He is describing a very old Negro woman in *The Sound and the Fury* (the title itself comes from Shakespeare's *Macbeth*, the source of the *multitudinous seas* passage). She has been fat, but now she is wrinkled and completely shrunken except for her stomach:

> . . . a paunch almost dropsical, as though muscle and tissue had been courage or fortitude which the days or the years had consumed until only the indomitable skeleton was left rising like a ruin or a landmark above the somnolent and impervious guts . . . .

The impact of that short, ugly Anglo-Saxon word, with its slang metaphorical pun, is almost unbearably moving. And the impact would be nothing, the effect slurring, without the grand Latin preparation. "What we need is a mixed diction."

Beware of wordiness. Verbosity is a disease. Symptoms: severe inflation of the language, difficulty in following the point, extreme drowsiness. Cause: too much Latin and the passive voice (see pp. 48–52). Cure: making words count, and administering moderate doses of Anglo-Saxon. In speaking of sentences earlier, I commended elaboration. But I also recommended deletion. A fully worded sentence, each word in place and pulling its weight, is a joy to see. But a sentence full of words is not. Words should count, I say again. And the best way to make them count is to count the words in each suspicious case. Any shorter version will be clearer. I once counted the words, sentence by sentence, in a thirty-page manuscript rejected as "too loose." In some sentences, I cut no more than one or two words. I rephrased many, but I think I cut no entire sentence. In fact, I added a considerable paragraph; and I still had five pages fewer, and a better essay.

Sentences can be too short and dense, of course. Many thoughts need explanation and an example or two. Many need the airing of *and*'s and *of*'s. Many simply need some loosening of phrase. In fact, colloquial phrasing, which is as clear and unnoticed as a clean window, is usually longer than its formal equivalent: *something to eat* as compared to *dinner*. By all counts, *dinner* should be better. It is shorter. It is more precise. Yet *something to eat* has social delicacy (at least as I am imagining the party). "Shall we have something to eat?" is more friendly than the more economical "Shall we have dinner?" We don't want to push our friends around with precise and economic suggestions. We want them at their ease, with the choices slightly vague. Consequently, when we write *what we are after* for *object* and *how it is done* for *method*, we give our all-too-chilly prose some social warmth. These colloquial phrases take more words, but they are not wordy if they pull with the rest of the sentence.

It all comes down to redundancy, the clutter of useless words and tangential ideas—"the accumulation of words that add nothing to the sense and cloud up what clarity there is," as Aristotle says. What we write should be easy to read. Too many distinctions, too many nouns, and too much Latin can be pea soup:

> Reading is a processing skill of symbolic reasoning sustained by the interfacilitation of an intricate hierarchy of substrata factors that have been mobilized as a psychological working system and pressed into service in accordance with the purpose of the reader.

This comes from an educator, with the wrong kind of education. He is saying:

> Reading is a process of symbolic reasoning aided by an intricate network of ideas and motives.

Try *not* to define your terms. If you do, you are probably either evading the toil of finding the right word, or defining the obvious:

> Let us agree to use the word "signal" as an abbreviation for the phrase "the simplest kind of sign." (This agrees fairly well with the customary meaning of the word "signal.")

Now, really! That came from a renowned semanticist, a student of the meanings of words. The customary meaning of a word *is* its meaning, and uncustomary meanings come only from careful punning. Don't underestimate your readers, as this semanticist did.

The definer of words is usually a bad writer. Our semanticist continues, trying to get his signals straight and grinding out about three parts sawdust to every one of meat. In the following excerpt, the italics are his; the brackets, mine. Read the sentence first as it was written; then read it again, omitting the bracketed words:

> The moral of such examples is that *all intelligent criticism* [*of any instance*] *of language* [*in use*] *must begin with understanding* [*of*] *the motives* [*and purposes*] *of the speaker* [*in that situation*].

Here, each of the bracketed phrases is already implied in the others. Attempting to be precise, the writer has beclouded himself. Naturally, the speaker would be "in that situation"; naturally, a sampling of language would be "an instance" of language "in use." *Motives* may not be *purposes,* but the difference here is insignificant. Our semanticist's next sentence deserves some kind of immortality. He means "Muddy language causes trouble":

> Unfortunately, the type of case that causes trouble in practice is that in which the kind of use made of language is not transparently clear . . . .

Clearly, transparency is hard. Writing is hard. It requires constant attention to meanings, and constant pruning. It requires a diction a cut above the commonplace, a cut above the inaccuracies and circumlocutions of speech, yet within easy reach. Clarity is the first aim; economy, the second; grace, the third; dignity, the fourth. Our writing should be a little strange, a little out of the ordinary, a little beautiful, with words and phrases not met every day but seeming as right and natural as grass. A good diction takes care and cultivation.

It can be overcultivated. It may seem to call attention to itself rather than to its subject. Suddenly we are aware of the writer at work, and a little too pleased with himself, reaching for the elegant cliché and the showy phrase, as if he were watching his gestures in a mirror. In the following passage, I have italicized elements inoffensive, or even effective, in themselves, but horribly mannered when they get together. Some are redundant; some are trite. Everything is somehow cozy and grandiose, and a little too nautical. Note the final, glorious fragment.

There's little excitement *ashore* when merchant ships from *faraway* India, Nationalist China, or Egypt *knife through* the *gentle swells* of Virginia's Hampton Roads. This *unconcern* may simply reflect the *nonchalance* of people who live by *one of the world's great seaports.* Or perhaps *it's just* that *folk* who *dwell* in the *home towns* of atomic submarines and Mercury astronauts are not likely to be impressed by a visiting freighter, *from however distant a realm.* An apprentice seaman aboard one of these *vessels soon learns* that he is entering *no sleepy southern harbor.* Around him in *the Roads* itself *ride* naval vessels of many nations, *perhaps including his own.* The big gray warships *dwarf* the *tiny* sailing *craft* and motor boats that *dart* around the water *on a good day. Off to port lies* Norfolk, *home* of the largest naval operating base *on this globe,* NATO's North Atlantic headquarters. *Upstream a bit* and also *to port,* the mouth of the Elizabeth River leads to Portsmouth and a major naval shipyard. *To starboard lies* Hampton, where at Langley Air Force Base the National Aeronautics and Space Administration prepares to send a man *into the heavens.* Just beyond Hampton *looms* the *huge* steel framework of the Newport News Shipbuilding and Dry Dock Company, *from whose ways slide* the atom-powered surface and underseas warships *of tomorrow. All this and more* form today's *metropolitan complex* surrounding Hampton Roads—four large, booming cities *peopled* by more than a million *souls*. *It's* a *huge, sprawling* urban area, *engaged* more than ever in world commerce and *deeply involved* in the nation's defense. *Here is the resurgent south, making instead of awaiting its destiny,* a hundred years and *a world away* from the *day* when the Monitor and the Merrimac *battled clumsily* in Hampton Roads. And still further away in time, *if not entirely in temper,* from the *geographically nearby restored* Colonial Capital at Williamsburg, from Captain John Smith's Jamestown Island, from the Yorktown battlefield on which George Washington *accepted the sword of surrender* from Cornwallis. °

SPELLING

Learn to spell the words you use. Spelling will increase your vocabulary and your grasp of meanings, as you spell out the meaningful parts. But everyone misspells a few old favorites—until fed up with himself. The dictionary is your best friend, in the presence of your enemies, but three underlying principles and some tricks of the trade can help immeasurably:

PRINCIPLE I . Letters represent sounds: proNUNciation can help you spell. No one proNOUNcing his words would make the familiar errors of "similiar" and "enviorment." You can even improve your social standing by learning to say *envIRONment* and *goverNment* and *FebRUary* and *intRAmural*. Simply sound out the letters. You can even say "convert*i*ble" and "indel*i*ble" and "plaus*i*ble" without sounding like a fool, and you can silently stress the *able* in words like "prob*able*" and "immov*able*" to remember the difficult distinction between words ending in *-ible,* and *-able.*

Consonants reliably represent their sounds. Remember that *c* and *g* go soft before *i* and *e*. Consequently you must add a *k* when extending words like *picnic* and *mimic—picnicKing, mimicKing—* to keep them from rhyming with *slicing* or *dicing*. Conversely, you just keep the *e* (where you would normally drop it) when making *peace* into *peacEable* and *change* into *changEable.*

Single *s* is pronounced *zh* in words like *vision, occasion, plea-*

° Robert Damron, "Hampton Roads," *Voyager,* July–August, 1960, p. 124.

sure. Knowing that *ss* hisses, or hushes, will keep you from errors like *occassion,* which would sound like *passion.*

Vowels sound short and light before single consonants: *hat, pet, mit, hop, mut.* When you add any vowel (including *y*), the first vowel will say its name: *hate, Pete, mite, hoping, mutable.* Notice how the *a* in *-able* keeps the main vowel saying its name in words like *unmistakable, likable,* and *notable.* Therefore, to keep a vowel short, protect it with a double consonant: *petting, hopping.* This explains the troublesome *rr* in *occuRRence:* a single *r* would make it say *cure* in the middle. *Putting* a golf ball and *putting* something on paper must both use *tt* to keep from being pronounced *pewting.* Compare *stony* with *sonny* and *bony* with *bonny.* The *y* is replacing the *e* in *stone* and *bone,* and the rule is working perfectly. It works in any accented syllable: compare *forgeTTable* with *markeTing,* and *begiNNing* with *buttoNing,* and *compeLLing* with *traveLing.*

Likewise, when *full* combines and loses its stress, it also loses an *l.* Note the single and double *l* in *fulFILLment.* Similarly, SOUL*ful,* GRATE*ful,* AW*ful*—even SPOON*ful.*

P R I N C I P L E   I I . This is the old rule of *i* before *e,* and its famous exceptions:

> **I before *e***
> **Except after *c,***
> **Or when sounded like *a***
> **As in *neighbor* and *weigh.***

It works like a charm (*achieve, believe; receive, conceive*). Note that *c* needs an *e* to make it sound like *s.* Remember also that *leisure* was once pronounced "lay-sure," and *foreign,* "for-ayn." Memorize these important exceptions: *seize, weird, either, sheik, forfeit, counterfeit.* Note that all are pronounced "ee" (with a little crowding) and that the *e* comes first. Then note that another small group goes the opposite way, having a long *i* sound as in the German "Heil": *height, sleight, seismograph, kaleidoscope.* Financier, another exception, follows its French origin and its original sound.

P R I N C I P L E   I I I . Most big words, following the Latin or French from which they came, spell their sounds letter for letter. Look up the derivations of the words you misspell (note that double *s*, and explain it). You will never again have trouble with *desperate* and *separate*, once you discover that the first comes from *de-spero*, "without hope," and that sePARate divides equals, as the PAR values in stocks or golf. Nor with *definite* or *definitive* once you see the kinship of both with *finite* and *finish*. Derivations can also help you a little with the devilment of *-able* and *-ible*, since, except for a few ringers, the *i* remains from Latin, and the *-ables* are either French (*ami-able*), or Anglo-Saxon copies (*work-able*). Knowing origins can help at crucial points: *resemblAnce* comes from Latin *simulAre*, "to copy"; *existEnce* comes from Latin *existEre*, "to stand forth." Similarly, you can link your unaccented errors with their accented relatives: *hypocrisy-hypocrite, irritable-irritate.*

The biggest help comes from learning the common Latin prefixes, which by assimilation (*ad-similis*, "like to like") account for the double consonants at the first syLLabic joint of so many of our words:

AD- (toward, to): *abbreviate* (shorten down), *accept* (grasp to).

CON- (with): *collapse* (fall with), *commit* (send with).

DIS- (apart): *dissect* (cut apart), *dissolve* (loosen apart).

IN- (into): *illuminate* (shine into), *illusion* (playing into).

IN- (not): *illegal* (not lawful), *immature* (not ripe).

INTER- (between): *interrupt* (break between), *interrogate* (ask between).

OB- (towards, to): *occupy* (take in), *oppose* (put to), *offer* (carry to).

SUB- (under): *suffer* (bear under), *suppose* (put down).

SYN- (together—this one is Greek): *symmetry* (measuring together), *syllogism* (logic together).

Spelling takes a will, an eye, and an ear. And a dictionary. Keep a list of your favorite enemies. Memorize one or two a day. Write them in the air in longhand. Visualize them. Imagine a blinking neon sign, with the wicked letters red and tall—d e f i n I t e— d e f i n I t e. Then print them once, write them twice, and blink them a few times more as you go to sleep. But best of all, make up whatever devices you can—the crazier the better—to remember the tricky parts:

DANCE attenDANCE.

EXISTENCE is TENSE.

LOOSE as a goose.

LOSE loses an o.

There's IRON in this enVIRON-
ment.
The resISTANCE took its STANCE.
There's an ANT on the defend-
ANT.

ALLOT isn't A LOT.
Already isn't ALL RIGHT.
I for gaiety.
The LL in paraLLel gives me *el*.
PURr in PURSuit.

Here are some more of the perpetual headaches:

accept—except
accommodate
acknowledgment—judgment
advice—advise
affect—effect
allusion—illusion—disillusion
analysis—analyzing—annual
apologize—Apollo
arrangement—argument
businessman
capital—capitol
careful—successful—fulfillment
challenge
cite—site—insight
committee
complement—compliment
council—counsel—consul
curriculum—career—occur-
rence
decide—divide—devices
desert—dessert
despair—desperate—separate

detrimental—dealt
dilemma—condemn
disastrous
embarrassment
eminent—imminent—immanent
exaggerate
explanation
forward—foreword
genius—ingenious
height—eighth
hypocrisy—democracy
irritable
lonely—loneliness
Negroes—heroes—tomatoes
obstacle
operate (opus, opera)
possession
primitive
principal—principle
proceed—precede—procedure
until—till

Check your capitals. You know about sentences and names,
certainly; but the following points are troublesome. Capitalize:

1. Names of races and languages—Negro, Indian, French,
English.

2. North, south, east, and west ONLY WHEN THEY ARE REGIONS
—the mysterious East, the new Southwest.

3. The COMPLETE names of churches, rivers, hotels, and the
like—the First Baptist Church, the Mark Hopkins Hotel, the
Suwannee River (not First Baptist church, Mark Hopkins hotel,
Suwannee river).

4. All words in titles, except prepositions, articles, and con-

junctions. But capitalize even these if they come first or last, or if they are longer than five letters—"I'm Through with Love," *Gone with the Wind*, "I'll Stand By," *In Darkest Africa*. Capitalize nouns, adjectives, and prefixes in hyphenated compounds—*The Eighteenth-Century Background*, *The Anti-Idealist* (but *The Anti-slavery Movement*). With magazines and newspapers only, drop the *The* as part of the title (the *Saturday Evening Post*, the Kansas City *Star*—note that only *Star*, or *Tribune*, or *Times* is treated as the newspaper's proper title).

5. References to a specific section of a work—the Index, his Preface, Chapter 1, Act II, Scene iii, Volume IV.

6. Abstract nouns, when you want emphasis, serious or humorous—". . . the truths contradict, so what is Truth?"; Very Important Person; the Ideal.

DO NOT capitalize the seasons—spring, winter, midsummer.

DO NOT capitalize after a colon, unless what follows is normally capitalized.

E X E R C I S E S

1. Browse your dictionary and find half a dozen families of words, like *ramp-rampage-rampant*. Give the root-idea of each family, and a short definition of each word, using the root-idea.

2. Make a permanent reference list by looking up in your dictionary each of the Latin and Greek prefixes and constituents listed below. Illustrate each with several English derivatives closely translated, as in these two examples: *con-* (*with*)—convince (conquer with), conclude (shut with), concur (run with); *gyno-* (*woman*)—gynephobia (fear of women), gynecocracy (government by women).

> LATIN: *a-* (*ab-*), *ad-*, *ante-*, *bene-*, *bi-*, *circum-*, *con-*, *contra-*, *di-* (*dis-*), *e-* (*ex-*), *in-* (two meanings), *inter-*, *intra-*, *mal-*, *multi-*, *ob-*, *per-*, *post-*, *pre-*, *pro-*, *retro-*, *semi-*, *sub-* (*sur-*), *super-*, *trans-*, *ultra-*.

> GREEK: *a-* (*an-*), *-agogue*, *allo-*, *anthropo-*, *anti-*, *apo-*, *arch-*, *auto-*, *batho-*, *bio-*, *cata-*, *cephalo-*, *chron-*, *-cracy*, *demo-*, *dia-*, *dyna-*, *dys-*, *ecto-*, *epi-*, *eu-*, *-gen*, *geo-*, *-gon*, *-gony*, *graph-*, *gyn-*, *hemi-*, *hepta-*, *hetero-*, *hexa-*, *homo-*, *hydr-*, *hyper-*, *hypo-*, *log-*, *mega-*, *meter-*, *micro-*, *mono-*, *morph-*, *-nomy*, *-nym-*, *-pathy*, *penta-*, *-phag*, *phil-*, *-phobe*(*ia*), *-phone*, *poly-*, *pseudo-*, *psyche-*, *-scope*, *soph-*, *stero-*, *sym*(*n*)*-*, *tele-*, *tetera-*, *theo-*, *thermo-*, *tri-*, *zoo-*.

3. Think up and look up eight or nine words built on each of the following Latin verbs and their past participles:

agere, actus (do)—agent, act

audire, auditus (hear)—audit

caedere, cisus (cut, cut down)—precise

capere, captus (seize)—capable

cedere, cessus (go)—concede

claudere, clausus (shut)—close, include

currere, cursus (run)—recur, course

dicere, dictus (say)—dictate

ducere, ductus (lead)—produce

facere, factus (make)—infect

ferre, latus (carry)—infer, relate

fidere, fisus (trust)—confide, Fido

fundere, fusus (pour)—refuse, refund

gerere, gestus (bear, act)—belligerent, gesture

gradi, gressus (step)—grade, digressions

ire, itus (go)—exit, tradition

jacere, jactus (throw)—reject

legere, lectus (choose, read)—legible, elect

loqui, locutus (speak)—circumlocution

mittere, missus (send)—permit, mission

pellere, pulsus (drive)—impel, repulse

pendere, pensus (hang)—depend, pension

plicare, plicatus (fold)—implication, complex

ponere, positus (put)—response, position

portare, portatus (carry)—import

rumpere, ruptus (break)—rumpus, erupt

scribere, scriptus (write)—scribble, script

sedere, sessus (sit)—sedentary, assess

sentire, sensus (feel)—sense

specere, spectus (look)—speculate

tendere, tensus (stretch)—tend, tense

tenere, tentus (hold)—content

trahere, tractus (drag)—tractor

venire, ventus (come)—convene, invent

vertere, versus (turn)—diverting, verse

videre, visus (see)—divide, visible

vocare, vocatus (call)—vocation

4. Capitalize the following, and italicize where necessary:

go west, young man.	she loved the spring.
the east side of town	health within seconds (book)
east side, west side	the missouri river

the methodist episcopal church	the tall negro spoke french. the country gentleman (mag-
the logical-positive approach (book)	azine) the st. louis post-dispatch
the new york public library	(newspaper)

5. Make five series of words running from particular to general, as in *ripe peach, peach, drupaceous fruit, fruit, dessert, food, nourishment.*

6. Make five series of words running from low connotations to high (see pp. 89, 95), drawing a line (when possible) where the Anglo-Saxon gives way to French or Latin. Start with *swine* and *stuck up* (meaning *conceited*). The abstract ideas will work best, and Roget's *Thesaurus* can be most helpful.

7. Write five sentences in which you use a concrete object to represent an entire abstract class, each sentence paired with its abstracted translation:

A *good steak* might have saved John Keats.
A *proper protein diet* might have saved John Keats.

8. Write five sentences in which you extend the metaphorical picture in common phrases such as *pin down, stick to, outline, count your chickens* ("She pinned him down methodically, each question sticking in a different place, until he couldn't wiggle out of it").

9. In your next essay, use a tactful *sweet as a nut, sharp as a tack,* and so forth, once on every page (see "Clichés," p. 149).

10. Write five sets of sentences illustrating the four levels of metaphor (see p. 92).

11. Write five sentences in which you revive a dead metaphor.

12. Write five sentences in which you pun metaphorically on a Latin word: "The *enterprise grabbed* everything"; His *introspection looked in* too keenly." Browsing your dictionary will help you here.

13. Write five sentences in which you couple a Latin adjective and an Anglo-Saxon noun, as in the phrase *inconsequential snip.*

9. Three Excursions

THE SEMESTER is now perhaps half over. Very likely you have been writing an essay a week, with exercises in between. You and your instructor are running out of ideas. Now is the time for greener pastures, before the harvest of the research paper. I propose three vacations without leaving the expository area. Each will tone up different linguistic muscles.

THE AUTOBIOGRAPHICAL ESSAY

The problem in this autobiographical excursion will be two-fold: first, to demonstrate a point; second, to describe accurately and vividly a personal experience. You will find yourself writing metaphorically as you try to bring to the reader exactly what your adventure was like. The aim of the exercise is to refresh your language with a dip into the descriptive, that stream of specific sights, sounds, feelings, and figurative comparisons into which regularly expository writing rarely ventures.

You will be telling an anecdote. And it must be interesting. Anecdotes are interesting only when they demonstrate some old truth about existence, when they offer an example of "they'll do it every time," sharpened to philosophical precision. Your tale may be comic or tragic. Look for the kind you would tell about yourself, or *on* yourself, to the young lady on your right at dinner. It must have a point, or her smile will be thin. For your essay, *cherchez la pointe*.

Suppose this is your proposition: "Pride goeth before a fall." You have in mind the time you were skating—capering and swooping for admiration, farther and farther, till the ice broke. With no thought at all, you would have known that it would make good conversation. In using it for your essay, you need more thought, more clarity, and more structure. You need a thesis. You need a beginning, a middle, and an end.

As always, devise your thesis first: "The old saying about pride's inviting a fall can prove disastrously true." Now, as always, crank back for your opening sentence. Keep *yourself* out of the beginning paragraph, at least until just before the thesis. You are not really writing about yourself. You are writing an essay about something generally true: you will be illustrating the general proposition with a personal experience, but the general truth is your point. Your beginning paragraph might look like this:

> No one believes that his parents know much. We are all sure that we know better, that all the old warnings are plots to curtail enjoyment, that all old sayings are relics of the Puritans. The parental warning, moreover, seems a gross underestimation of our powers and maturity. We are insulted; we have been treated as children. This resentful pride, these illusions of manhood, are woefully normal, and undoubtedly behind most of the evening paper's reports of catastrophes befalling the young. This seems to be the way we are made, and all of us are lucky if we escape bodily harm from our own arrogance. The old saying about pride's going before a fall can prove disastrously true.

Now for the middle. This tells the story. Your entire episode comes in to illustrate your thesis:

> I learned this one sunny winter afternoon. Five of us, close friends since first grade, had eaten lunch at my house, three blocks from the Willawee River. We had been obstreperous. My mother had been harried and amused as she made more sandwiches, more hot chocolate, and scraped out the last of the pudding. "Now, be careful," she had said as we started to get our things together on the porch. "Now, be careful," I mimicked to the others, feeling too good for thought. She called me into the hall and dressed me down. "Just remember that pride goes before a fall," she said. How I hated that old saying. My grandmother always managed to work it in at least once a visit. As I turned to go, my mother added in a completely different tone: "Please don't go out too far, John. Remember the Simmons boy."
>
> I remembered nothing as I walked away with my grinning

companions—except my resentment, a small dull twist in my stomach, even after the bright afternoon had lifted all of us again to our lunchtime heights. The air was like alcohol on the skin. Everything sparkled in the clear air; everything seemed closer than normal. The river looked like frosting, but down the middle a dull green vein straggled.

And so, on to the climax, which now threatens to be tragic. You, of course, would know how it ended, because your experience, unlike the one above, would have been real.

The value of the exercise depends on your using a real experience. This demands of your powers something more than logical progressions. This asks you not to think up a subject and think out its consequences, but to render as truly and particularly as possible a subject already there, something you have experienced but perhaps have never put into words, have never fully conveyed to someone else. It asks you to gather the half-remembered circumstances into a picture very like what they were, a picture that will show your readers how it was. You could tell the whole thing in three sentences: "I dared Bill to follow. We fell in. He froze and drowned." But you need to do what every storyteller must do: keep from telling the story, keep it from ending, while neither losing your reader's interest nor trying his patience. You need detail and detail and detail, simile after simile after metaphor, to postpone the climax and to let us see and feel how it was.

The ending may be no more than a sentence, or it may be a ruminative paragraph, generalizing upward and outward from the particulars to mirror the beginning paragraph, as in a regular essay. The dramatic curve of your incident will tell you what to do. It may be well to end when the story has told itself out, and made its point starkly: "The four of us walked numbly up the street toward home."

THE TERRIBLE ESSAY

Now that you have made an excursion into figurative language, and have seen what concrete words can do, you will go on a treasure hunt for the horrendously abstract. Nothing can be more salutary. You will work out all the fever. Again we follow the essay's form, this time in parody not only of the form itself, but especially of that abstract lint the bad essay uses for language. You write the worst essay you can think of.

First, some rules.

1. Use no other verb but *is*. Rule 2 will then be easy.

2. Put EVERYTHING in the passive voice.

3. Use no adjectives; use nouns instead. An *excellent idea* becomes *the conception of an excellence program*. Do not say *governmental spending;* say *government spending*.

4. Use no participles; use verbs with *which:* not *dripping,* but *which drip*.

5. Use only one adverb, frequently repeated, and pick a good big cloudy one like *considerably* or *indubitably*—nothing like *sharply,* or *painfully,* or *crazily,* or *happily*.

6. Use only big abstract nouns—as many *-tion*'s as possible.

7. Use plenty of *which*'s.

8. String out your sentences in festoons of three or more prepositional phrases, each with the same preposition—especially *of*.

9. Use as many words as possible to say the least. Say "It has been considerably in evidence for a considerable period of time that something is in a state of putrefaction in one of the most time-honored and revered of Nordic commonwealths and principalities" instead of "Something is rotten in the state of Denmark" (even Shakespeare could use a few words too many).

10. Work in as many trite expressions as possible: *Needless to say, all things being equal, in the foreseeable future, a better world in which to live, due to the fact that, in terms of, various and sundry.*

11. Sprinkle heavily with *-wise*-type and *type*-type expressions.

12. Say *hopefully* every three or four sentences.

13. Compile a basic vocabulary: *situation, aspect, function, factor, phase, utilize, the use of, -type, -wise,* and so on. The class may well cooperate in this.

As with all rules, you can sometimes break these to good effect. Were you to follow them meticulously you would be unintelligible. What you want is a parody of badness, with enough goodness to make it fun. Your project will be an ultra-serious study of trivia. I propose: *A Report of a Study of the Person Sociology and Night*

Loss Cost Economics of the Faucets Which Drip in the Second Floor North Corner Woman Dormitory Lavatory.
    Now write a good bad beginning paragraph:

> The necessity of cleanliness is considerably in evidence to every individual who is concerned in the creation of a better world in which to live. Water is necessary to be utilized as a maintenance factor in the health functioning of all human-type beings. Hopefully, it will not be denied that young women which are classified as beings of the college-type category should not be excluded from consideration in this connection. As a consequence of this nature-life principle, which is a major aspect of the situation, every dormitory situated on the property of the campus of the University of Blank has been provided with a number of examples of lavatories which are of a tile-chromium nature. They have the appearance of being adequate, hopefully, and of being the finalized result of an investment utility program of an economy-necessity nature. However, careful investigation of the science objective type has disclosed a large number of factors operative phasewise, the chief of which is that of a number of chromium fixture lavatory faucets which function in a manner not in accordance with economy or utility. All things being equal, they drip. The present study is hopefully an examination of lavatation in terms of a representative example, and features the inclusion of conclusions in regard to confusion between a water waste compulsion type individual and a drip.

With ingenuity you can keep this going throughout your essay, filling out a sober middle with statistics and an elegant end with pomp.

THE IRONIC ESSAY

Your Terrible Essay has, of course, been ironic. In it, you have feigned an appearance contrary to reality. To spoof the errors of earnest professionalism, you have pretended to be an earnest professional. You have practiced one kind of verbal irony, making your words mean the opposite of what they say. They have appeared to say "This is serious and important"; they have really said that all of it—with the whole mode of vanity it represents—is nonsense. You have proceeded, moreover, with a perfect understanding that your reader sees the pose and is enjoying it with you.

The first requirement for irony, then, is an understanding shared between author and reader. It is like Pig Latin, or any other secret language, in which two can talk and circumvent a third. It is, in William Empson's words, a way of getting by the censor. The pleasure in irony is the smuggler's pleasure. I can say, "It was a fine day"; the uninitiated will think it really was, but you and I will know that it was not. The pleasure in the secret, furthermore, gives the truth an emphasis beyond that of bald statement. Alongside irony, plain statement seems uncouth. "It was a terrible day" seems young and petulant. "It was a fine day" is the voice of refined experience, a suggestion of tweed and teacups, Tobruk to El Alamein, tigers in Bengal, and never a hair turned. A few of the guests might think the day's shooting had been good, but the speaker and you and I would know—and enjoy the unperturbed secret, even secretly enjoy the disappointment because it made irony possible—that the day had been terrible.

For your Ironic Essay, therefore, pick something that is common knowledge. The ironist does not write to one alone, but he writes to all his readers as if each were the only one, complimenting each on his perspicacity. If his subject is not generally and publicly important, he will be talking in riddles. He takes something of public interest—a proposal to raise taxes, for instance. He pretends to be pompous and nearsighted, as if he narrowly misconceives the issue and cannot see the full implications of his words. His pose will be much like yours in the Terrible Essay. He makes his pose the opposite of his true standpoint, at the same time making his true standpoint clear. He writes:

> The popular clamor against the proposed raise in taxes is as shortsighted as it is unfounded. Purging the purse is good for the spleen. What does it matter that the present Drain Commissioner has wasted exactly a half-million dollars on a poorly conceived plan? What does it matter that our fine city council now finds it necessary to ask for a new bond and a new assessment to overhaul a drainage system just four years old? It matters not. The moral discipline of digging deeper into the pocket so that the Commissioner may dig a deeper drain is good for the soul, even if we must all skip a meal now and then and take out a second mortgage. There is nothing like good drainage.

Or he writes:

> The public has again expressed its infinite wisdom in voting down the recent bond issue. Niggardliness is next to godliness, as my great-uncle used to say. It really does not matter that classrooms built for twenty are desperately trying to hold forty; nor that our best teachers are leaving for Southfield and Adams and Middlebranch, and even Potfield, simply because they can no longer teach the numbers of students pouring into our beautiful Smith School—one of our most revered landmarks, by the way, and certainly the oldest. If we can save enough for our beer and T.V. tubes, our children's education really does not matter. We're keeping them off the streets, aren't we?

This mixing of fact and irony exacts careful wording. The two examples above seek to keep clear the line between straight statement and ironic inversion. It does matter, the writer implies, that the local classrooms are crowded. It is true that they are crowded to almost twice their effective capacity; it is true that at least three good teachers have left for positions in Southfield, Adams, and Middlebranch, and that a fourth has even been lured away to dumpy Potfield. The writer calls the public wise and means foolish; yet he calls them niggardly and means niggardly. How does he do it?

The first clue is overstatement: *expressed its infinite wisdom* is a rotund circumlocution for *wise*, and *infinite wisdom* is a cliché. Then the language goes straight, and we know that the bond issue was, in fact, defeated. The tactics change in the next sentence. Here the writer calls a spade a spade but uses it as an argument for the opposition, making it a poor argument by the harshness of *niggardliness* and the absurdity of its new setting in the old proverb. He implies that the opposing arguments are just that poorly founded. The next sentence makes its irony clear when the facts of two-for-one crowding controvert the opening phrase, making it pure verbal irony: *it does not matter* means *it does matter*. And so on. *Beautiful* means *ugly*; the building is old and it is a landmark, all right, but if it is revered it is wrongly revered.

Now, the writer did not (as I think I can testify) ask himself "Is this an overstatement?" or "Is this an understatement?" or "Is this a cliché?" He simply had his point in mind, took the ironic stance, and struck the ironic tone. He allowed his language to inflate or to belittle (*it really does not matter*) as he went along, assuming the ironic pose, the ignorant pose, and dropping it when he wanted to go straight. He knows that his audience is with him, or that the secret appeal of irony will make them wish they were.

Your first step is to take some current campus issue, for which you will have a supporting audience. A topic that works well, because of its simplicity and perennial currency, is the state of dormitory food. Actually, dormitory food is not bad, but then it is not what mother used to make either. You can probably think of enough amusing detail to make you glad of the chance for irony its mediocrity affords. So: your real thesis is that dormitory food is horrible. Your ironic thesis, obviously, will be: "Dormitory food is absolutely delicious." Now, put on the blinkers; narrow your vision down to that one point. You cannot possibly understand how anyone can complain of such a splendid cuisine. Your first paragraph will go something like this:

THE DELICACIES OF THE SMITH HALL STEAMTABLE

One of man's perversities is to complain. Give him a new suit, and he complains that his neckties do not match. Give him a new car, and he complains about the size of his garage. Give a child wholesome food, and he complains that he does not like it. Food, in fact, is one of man's oldest complaints. Adam and Eve wearied of the bill of fare even in Paradise, and nothing in this world is better roughage than fruit and raw vegetables. We hear the same old story in Smith Hall. Give students paradise, and they want steak. Give them steak even as frequently as once a year, and they complain that it is thin or cold or dried out. The cuisine at the Smith Hall steamtable, as any educated palate can tell, is delicious; and though to a handful of dyspeptic latecomers it may seem cold and dry and unappetizing, it is nonetheless extremely well balanced: in fact, it never changes.

Now, if you wish, take this as your beginning paragraph, adjust it to your needs, and write on—through the satisfactions of cold mashed potatoes, plastic whipped cream, and gravied bus boys, not forgetting to fashion a rich and impassioned peroration as your end paragraph. Any other convenient local topic will do. The trick is to find the ironic stance and tone, and through irony to learn the dynamics in even the commonest words.

SUGGESTIONS FOR TOPICS

1. *The Autobiographical Essay.* An automobile accident, a harrowing experience as camp counselor, a family picnic, a party that flopped, the big date, a new friend who clung, a disappointing trip, a first week at college.

2. *The Terrible Essay.* Book borrowers, the habits of smokers, the way professors enter the classroom, library daydreamers, fashions in makeup, creaking doors, freshman composition.

3. *The Ironic Essay.* The joys of learning languages by tape, Chinese made easy, happy college days, the beloved roommate, the eight o'clock class, our courteous age, chivalry is not dead, the joys of cooking, college —the home away from home.

10. The Research Paper

Now to consolidate and advance. Instead of one thousand words, you will write three thousand. Instead of a self-propelled debate, you will write a scholarly argument. You will also learn to use the library, and to take notes and give footnotes. You will learn the manners of scholarship. You will learn to acknowledge your predecessors as you distinguish yourself, to make not only a bibliography, but a contribution.

The research paper is very likely not what you think it is. *Re*-search is searching again. You are looking, usually, where others have looked before; but your aim is to see something they have not seen. Research is not combining a paragraph from *The Encyclopaedia Britannica* and a paragraph from *The Book of Knowledge* with a slick pinch from *Life*. That's robbery. Nor is it research if you carefully change each phrase and acknowledge the source. That's drudgery. Even in some high circles, I am afraid, such scavenging is called research. It is not. It is simply a cloudier condensation of what you have done in school as a "report"— sanctioned plagiarism to teach something about ants or Ankara, a tedious compiling of what is already known. That such material is new to you is not the issue: it is already in the public stock.

Choosing Your Subject

Find a thesis. What, then, can you do, with things so well stocked? You move from facts to ideas. Here the range is infinite. Every old idea needs new assertion. Every new assertion needs judgment. Here you are in the area of value, and of values, where everyone is in favor of virtue but in doubt about what is virtuous.

Your research problem is to make a judgment of right or wrong on some controversial issue.

I have put it bluntly to save you from drowning in slips of paper. Remember that an opinion is not a private fancy; it is an opinion of what the right is, of what the truth is, of what the facts mean. It is a judgment of what *is*—out there somewhere, not merely in somebody's head. An opinion, when careful and informed, is as close as anyone will ever get to truth: a statement of what the truth of the matter seems to be. Your opinion may be just as accurate as anybody's, and the major task of the research paper is to sift opinions.

Your sifter, as always, is your thesis, right there at the neck of your beginning paragraph—which, as always, is your essay in miniature. Make your thesis first, *before you begin researching*. Call it a hypothesis (a "subthesis"), if that will make you comfortable. It does seem unscientific. But it is nearer the scientific method than it looks. The scientist, too, plays his hunches. James Watt saw the steam condenser in the lid of his aunt's teakettle; Donald Glaser saw the tracks of atomic particles in the bubbles of his beer. As with scientific experiment and the simple essay, if the hypothesis proves wrong, the testing will have furnished means to make it more nearly right. With the research paper, if you do not have a thesis to lead you through the twists and turns of print, you will never come out the other end. Unless you have a working hypothesis to keep your purpose alive as you collect, you may collect forever, forever hoping for a purpose. If you have a thesis, you will learn—and then overcome—the temptations of collecting only the supporting evidence and ignoring the obverse facts and whispers of conscience. If further facts and good arguments persuade you to the other side, so much the better. You will be the stronger for it.

Persuade your reader you are right. You do not search primarily for facts. You do not aim to summarize everything ever said on the subject. You aim to persuade your reader that the thesis you believe in is right. You persuade him by: (1) letting him see that you have been thoroughly around the subject and that you know what is known of it and thought of it, (2) showing him where the wrongs are wrong, and (3) citing the rights as right. *Your* opinion, *your* thesis, is what you are showing; all your quotations from all the authorities in the world are subservient to *your* demonstration. You are the reigning authority. You have, for the moment, the longest perspective and the last word.

Pick an argument.   The tactics of the research paper, then, are exactly those of any argumentative essay. Of course, you can give even straight exposition an argumentative edge: you can take as a subject not just "House Cats" but "House cats are more intelligent than most people realize." You can find something to prove even in straight description: "See," you say, "this has been overlooked; this has not been appreciated; this has been misunderstood." But you will be stronger yet in dealing with a controversial topic. Therefore: (1) pick a subject in which much is to be said on both sides; (2) take the side where your heart is; (3) write a thesis sentence with a *because* in it; (4) gather your material around and about the *pro* and *con;* (5) write an essay with beginning, middle, and end, and with a *pro*-and-*con* structure like one of those described on pages 12–13.

Pick something that interests you.   You need not shake the world. Such subjects as "Subsidized College Football," "Small College Versus Big University," or the worth of "A Best-Selling Novel" well suit the research paper—a three-fold elaboration of the simple essay involving: (1) the handling of your argument, (2) the citation of others' facts and arguments *as part of your own,* and (3) the managing of footnotes and bibliography. Bigger subjects, of course, will try your mettle: subjects like "The Rights of Slaveholders in the Old South," "Euthanasia," "Socialized Medicine." The whole question of governmental versus private endeavors affords many lively issues for research and decision—the ills and virtues of commercial television, for instance.

USING THE LIBRARY

Find the card catalogue.   Its 3 x 5 cards list all the library's holdings—books, magazines, newspapers, atlases—and alphabetize (1) authors, (2) publications, and (3) general subjects, from *A* to *Z.* John Adams and *The Anatomy of Melancholy* and Atomic Energy will be found, in that order, in the *A* drawers. The table on the next page shows the three kinds of cards (filed alphabetically) on which the card catalogue will list the same book—by author, by subject, and by title.

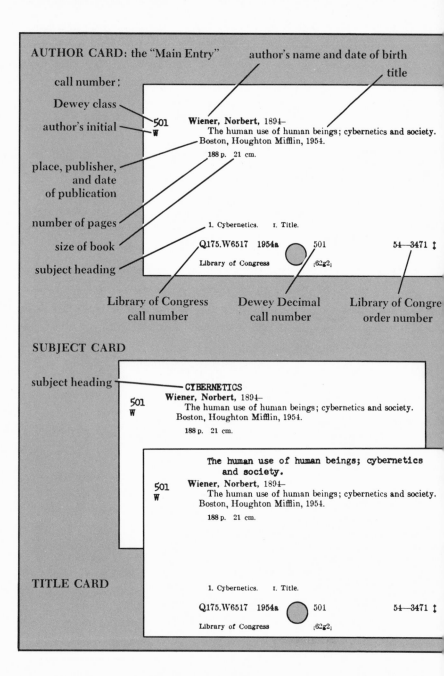

AUTHOR CARD: the "Main Entry"

author's name and date of birth

title

call number:

Dewey class

author's initial

501
W

Wiener, Norbert, 1894–
    The human use of human beings; cybernetics and society.
Boston, Houghton Mifflin, 1954.

188 p.   21 cm.

place, publisher,
and date
of publication

number of pages

size of book

subject heading

1. Cybernetics.   I. Title.

Q175.W6517   1954a

Library of Congress

501

[62g2]

54—3471 ‡

Library of Congress
call number

Dewey Decimal
call number

Library of Congre
order number

SUBJECT CARD

subject heading

501
W

CYBERNETICS
Wiener, Norbert, 1894–
    The human use of human beings; cybernetics and society.
Boston, Houghton Mifflin, 1954.

188 p.   21 cm.

501
W

The human use of human beings; cybernetics
    and society.
Wiener, Norbert, 1894–
    The human use of human beings; cybernetics and society.
Boston, Houghton Mifflin, 1954.

188 p.   21 cm.

TITLE CARD

1. Cybernetics.   I. Title.

Q175.W6517   1954a

Library of Congress

501

[62g2]

54—3471 ‡

You will notice that the bottom of the card shows the Library of Congress's cataloguing number (Q175.W6517) and the number from the older, but still widely used, Dewey Decimal System (501). Whichever one your library uses, that is the "call number" to put on your slip when you sign out the book.

Learn the catalogue's inner arrangements. Since some alphabetical entries run on drawer after drawer—New York City, New York *Times,* New York State, for instance—knowing the arrangements *within* these entries will help you find your book.

1. Not only men, but organizations and institutions, can be "authors" if they publish books or magazines, as do the following:

Parke, Davis & Company, Detroit
The University of Michigan
U.S. Department of State

2. Initial *A, An, The,* and their foreign equivalents (*Ein, El, Der, Une,* and so forth) are ignored in alphabetizing a title: *A Long Day in a Short Life* is alphabetized under *L.* But French surnames are treated as if they were one word: *De la Mare* as if *Delamare, La Rochefoucauld* as if *Larochefoucauld.*

3. Cards are usually alphabetized *word by word: Stock Market* comes before *Stockard* and *Stockbroker.* "Short before long" is another way of putting it, meaning that *Stock* and all its combinations with separate words precede the longer words beginning with *Stock-.* Hyphenations are treated as two words. The sequence would run thus:

Stock
Stock-Exchange Rulings
Stock Market
Stockard

4. Cards on one subject are arranged alphabetically by author. Under *Anatomy,* for instance, you will run from "Abernathy, John" to "Yutzy, Simon Menno," and then suddenly run into a title—*An Anatomy of Conformity*—which happens to be the next large alphabetical item after the subject, *Anatomy.*

5. Identical names are arranged in the order (a) persons, (b) titles and places as they fall alphabetically:

Washington, Booker T.
Washington, George

Washington (State)
Washington, D.C.
Washington, University of
Washington Square [by Henry James]

"Washington," the state, precedes "Washington, D.C." because "State" (which appears on the card only in parentheses) is not treated as part of its name.

6. Since *Mc, M',* and *Mac* are all filed as *Mac,* go by the letter following them: *M'Coy, McDermott, Machinery, MacKenzie.*

7. Other abbreviations are also filed as if spelled out: *Dr. Zhivago* would be filed as if beginning with *Doctor; St.* as if *Saint; Mrs. Miniver* as if *Mistress*—except that many libraries now alphabetize *Mr.* and *Mrs.* as spelled.

8. Saints, popes, kings, and people are filed, in that order, by name and not by appellation (do not look under *Saint* for St. Paul, nor under *King* for King Henry VIII):

Paul, Saint
Paul VI, Pope
Paul I, Emperor of Russia
Paul, Jean

9. An author's books are filed first by collected works, then by individual titles. Books *about* him then follow the books *by* him:

Fielding, Henry 1707–1754

The Works of Henry Fielding, esq.	1784
The Works of Henry Fielding, esq.	1806
The Complete Works of Henry Fielding	1840
Selections	1923
Amelia	1752
The History of Amelia	1857
The History of the Adventures of Joseph Andrews	1839
The History of Tom Jones, a foundling	1749
The History of Tom Jones, a foundling	1836
[works about]	
Allen, Walter, *Six Great Novelists*	

Notice that this library owns only a later edition of *Joseph Andrews,* printed long after the author's death in 1754.

THE PROCEDURES OF RESEARCH

Get the equipment, and gather the material. Now that you are somewhat familiar with the library, you are ready to dig into your own job of research. First, get some 3 × 5 cards for your bibliography, some 3 × 5 slips of paper for notes, and some kind of envelope to hold them. Since you will work up your bibliography first, you may find that your cards still have enough room on face and back for whatever notes you need. Since notes should be brief and few, the limits of your one bibliographical card per source may keep you trim. If you take several notes from each source, however, use your slips of paper and put only one note, even if only a phrase, on each slip. This will facilitate your shuffling and organizing. Plan on some ten or twenty sources for your 3,000 words of text. Make all entries, take all notes, in *ink*. After the thumbing, you will be thankful. You will fill out your cards as you find what you want in card catalogues and indexes. Italicize (that is, underline) titles of books and magazines; put titles of articles found *within* books and magazines in quotation marks. Your cards will look something like this:

BOOK

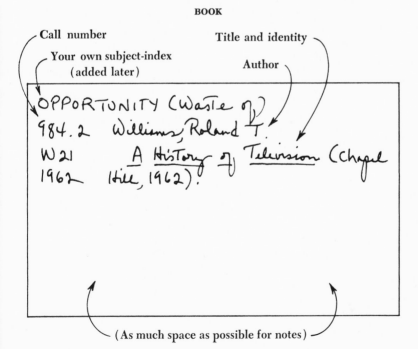

Call number

Your own subject-index
(added later)

Title and identity

Author

(As much space as possible for notes)

(You will, of course, add your subject-heading only after you have had a look at the book and found it useful.)

ARTICLE

> COSTS
> AP 3
> A 4
> (undergrad.
>   Stacks)
>
> Johnson, Paul Jr.
> "Three Thousand a Minute,"
> <u>American</u> <u>Nation</u>, XVI (June
> 1953), 319–333.

(This is old enough to be bound and in the stacks—hence the call number.)

NEWS STORY

> CONTROL
> AN
> 23
> .N5
> N 595
>
> "Commission Recommends T. V.
> Control," <u>New York Times</u>, Jan. 6,
> 1955, Sec. 1, p. 4.

You will check spellings, volume numbers, places, dates, and pages, when you finally get your magazine or book in hand, putting a light √ in pencil to assure yourself that your card is authoritative, safe to check your finished paper against. Get the author's name as he signed it, adding detail in brackets if helpful: D[elmar] P[rince] Smith. Get all the information; the sample foot-notes on pages 130 through 132 will show you what you may need, especially in complicated references.

Start with encyclopedias.   Now that you have located the card catalogue, find the *Encyclopaedia Britannica* and the *Readers' Guide to Periodical Literature,* and your problems are nearly solved. But begin with the *Britannica.* This will survey your subject (for latest news, see latest editions, and the annual supplementary "year books"). Each article will refer you, at the end, to several author-ities. If someone's initials appear at the end, look them up in the Contributors' List, or in the Index (the last volume of the set). The author is an authority himself; you should mention him in your paper. Furthermore, the Contributors' List will name several works, which will swell your bibliography and aid your research. The Index will also refer you to data scattered through all the volumes. Under "Medicine," for instance, it directs you to such topics as "Academies," "Hypnotism," "Licensing," "Mythology," and so on. Since the *Britannica* now revises progressively, subject by subject, note the date on the copyright page to see how much you may need to bring your subject up to date. The *Encyclopedia Americana and Collier's Encyclopedia,* though less celebrated, will here and there challenge *Britannica*'s reign. Others will help:

The American Yearbook
Catholic Encyclopedia
Columbia Encyclopedia
Cyclopedia of American Agriculture
Cyclopedia of American Government
Cyclopedia of Education
Commerce Yearbook
Dictionary of American Biography [abbreviated *DAB* in footnotes]
Dictionary of American History
Dictionary of the Bible
Dictionary of National Biography [British—abbreviated *DNB* in footnotes]

Dictionary of Philosophy and Psychology
Encyclopedia of Banking and Finance
Encyclopedia of Religion and Ethics
Encyclopedia of the Social Sciences
Encyclopedia of World Art
Encyclopedia of World History
Grove's Dictionary of Music and Musicians
Harper's Encyclopedia of Art
Hutchinson's Technical and Scientific Encyclopedia
Jewish Encyclopedia
The Statesman's Year-Book
Who's Who [British]
Who's Who in America

The World Almanac and Book of Facts, a paperbacked mine of news and statistics (issued yearly since 1868), can provide a factual nugget for almost any subject. The *Interpreter's Bible Dictionary* is another gold mine.

Comb the indexes. With your encyclopedic background sketched, go next to the card catalogue, then to the magazine indexes. Both use the same system, listing each work three times (alphabetically): by author, by title, and by subject. Izaak Walton's *Compleat Angler* would be listed under "Walton, Izaak" and under "*Compleat Angler*" and again under "Fishing," and a good index would also include "Angling—see Fishing." The index directs you around within itself rather well. So, for your research paper, simply take your subject and see what books your library lists under it. Two or three of the most recent books will probably give you all you want, because each of these, in turn, will refer you, by footnote and bibliography, to important previous works. Make your bibliographical cards as you go.

Now for the *Readers' Guide*—an index of articles (and portraits and poems) in more than one hundred magazines. Again, take the most recent issue, look up your subject, and make out your cards—spelling out the abbreviations of titles and dates according to the key just inside the cover. If you don't spell them out fully, your cards may be mysteries to you when you sit down to write. You can drop back a few issues and years to collect more articles; and if your subject belongs to the recent past (after 1907), you can drop back to the right year and track your subject forward.

You can do the same with *The New York Times Index,* beginning with 1913. It will probably lead you to news that appeared in any paper. The *Social Sciences and Humanities Index* does for the scholarly journals what the *Readers' Guide* does for the popular ones. Add to these the *Book Review Digest* and the *Biography Index* (which nicely collects scattered references), and you will probably need no more. But here are some others:

Annual Magazine Subject-Index [particularly for history]
Art Index
Dramatic Index
Education Index
Engineering Index
Essay and General Literature Index [very useful for locating particular subjects within collections of essays]
Index Medicus
Industrial Arts Index [for business and technical subjects]
International Catalogue of Scientific Literature
Music Index
Psychological Index
Public Affairs Information Service [valuable for "current events" beginning with October 15, 1914]
Technical Book Review Index

If you need more, consult Constance M. Winchell's *Guide to Reference Books.*

Take few notes. Now, first the books, then the magazines. With cards in hand, begin with a likely-looking book. Read quickly, with an eye for the general idea, and the telling point. Having a clear thesis will guide your note-taking. You can be sparing and spare. Some of your sources will need notes no fuller than "Violently opposed; recommends complete abolition." This violent and undistinguished author will appear in your paper only among several others in a single footnote to one sentence: "Opposition, of course, has been long and emphatic.[2]" Now is the time, too, to put a *pro* or a *con* in the upper right corner of your card.

Your next source, however, turns out to have something substantial to say, though still in opposition. This man writes well enough to be quoted. A *con* will put him in his place; a summary phrase will cover him: "Bases argument entirely on practical grounds, sets moral issue aside as irrelevant and 'Utopian.' " Now, within exaggerated quotation marks, put down the sentence or two you want. Your card would look like this:

Take care with page numbers. Notice how I have put "214" where the quotation turns the page—I might want to use only part of the excerpt and then be uncertain as to which of the two pages held it. Notice also how I have used brackets around my own words, just to make sure that I don't later confuse them with quoted material. Check your quotation against the original, word for word, and give it a penciled check when you know it is accurate.

Use your slips of paper only if you feel you need more notes than these. Put a "2" in the upper right corner of your first slip; copy and summarize away, using brackets and big quotation marks and putting page numbers in parentheses right where they belong. At the bottom of the slip note the author and page numbers ("Adamson, 215–17"), and start slip 3, if you must. When all your notes are taken, you are ready to write.

THE FIRST DRAFT

Start to plan your paper by writing a beginning paragraph. Formal outlines, especially those made too early in the game, can take more time than they are worth, but a long paper with notes demands some planning. First, draft a beginning paragraph, incorporating your thesis:

THE CASE FOR SOCIALIZED TELEVISION

Freedom for all is the essential idea in a democracy; and free enterprise, it is often said, has made America strong. From the first we have resisted governmental controls, throwing tea into Boston harbor and overthrowing British rule. To this day, "Big Government" usually spells "bad government" to most people, suggesting dictators, inhuman regimentation and terror, and societies of robots. Freedom for the individual is our belief and our goal. But the idea also involves freedom of opportunity, and here, I think, "Big Government" can function, as it has functioned in the past, to prevent one man's enterprise from seizing another man's opportunity. Some such seizure has taken place in the television enterprises of the United States. A brief comparison with the British system, and a little thought, will show that the United States Government could control television with no real damage to free enterprise and with a great widening of opportunity for all. American television is not living up to its opportunities.

Canvass your notes and plot your course. Read them through, sorting them into three piles: *pro's, con's,* and *in-between's* (often simply facts). Now, by way of outline, make three or four general headings on a sheet of paper, with ample space between. Let us assume a complex *pro-and-con* structure. Under each of your headings, make a list of the *con's* against a list of your *pro's,* as they seem to mount and to balance each other. Start with a list of insignificant *con's,* to be finished in a sentence, and move to the more significant. Your sketch will look something like this:

I. Commercial argument—Gov't would still leave room for advertising

Pro	*Con*
	Allenberg
	Hawkins, Weiss
	Smith
	Dillon
	Jones (p. 20)
But—Jones (p. 23)	
Lecky's facts	
N.Y. Times	
Cummings	

II. Educational argument (as against "Entertainment")

<table>
<tr><td align="center">Pro</td><td align="center">Con</td></tr>
<tr><td></td><td align="center">Perkins</td></tr>
</table>

But—Brown (hrs./day that
children watch)

Facts {
Johnson
Flemming
Steinberg
Lane
}

III. Freedom to choose—Collins, Williams, Thos. Jefferson's "aristocracy of talent."

IV. Opportunity to learn and to be amused—Wilkins.

Notice, first, that your references are thick at first and thin toward the end. As I have said, you will handle each of the first four or five *con*'s in a sentence or two; the rest will get more space. But with Perkins's protests you will leave the *con* side altogether, well before you are halfway through. You will still be citing and quoting under heading III, but these men will all be on your side; and in section IV you will be entirely on your own, except for one stirring quotation from Wilkins.

Put in your references as you go. Your first draft should have all your footnotes, abbreviated, right in the text. Otherwise you will lose your place, and go mad with numbers. Put the notes at the *end* of the last pertinent sentence, with as many of your references as possible grouped in one note. Make your quotations in full, and include the author's surname and the page number with each citation. You will change these in your final draft, of course, filling in the names or leaving them out of the note altogether if they appear in the text. But it will help you in checking against your cards to have an author's name and a page number for each citation. *Don't number your footnotes yet.* When your draft is finished, add the numbers in pencil, so you can change them; circled in red, so you can see them (a red pencil is really worth its price). As you type along, mark your notes with triple parentheses: (((. . .)))— the easiest distinction you can make. Check the rules about quotation marks on pages 83 and 84 (you should single-space and indent all *long* quotations). Now, settle down to the keyboard and begin your second paragraph.

Free enterprise and freedom of opportunity, of course, are the first appeals of those who defend American television as it now is. Any mention of governmental control, or even of change in the present system, is likely to be met with cries of "Socialism" and lectures on the American heritage. (((Allenberg, p. 10; Hawkins, p. 16; Weiss, p. 5; Smith, "This is creeping socialism. This is not the American way," p. 77))) Miles W. Dillon argues that the television networks must awake to their national responsibility in helping keep America free by "cleaning their own house," thus forestalling the governmental intrusion that will be a first step toward absolute governmental control, propaganda, and dictatorship. (((Dillon, pp. 23–25))) Bingham Jones, a proponent of mild governmental regulation, acknowledges these same dangers and concedes that the best solution would be a general renovation by the networks themselves. (((Jones, p. 20)))

But, Jones continues, the networks will never do it; the sponsors are too firmly entrenched:

> If the general housecleaning, so frequently recommended, so frequently attempted, could work, the entire problem would disappear. Our television systems would have arrested their slow deterioration. The lost adult audiences would have been regained . . . . We could again see great works of literature dramatized frequently; we could again explore the world with the informed camera and explore ideas with the best minds of the country. But so long as advertising agents select programs with sales their sole consideration, no house will be cleaned. Indeed, up to the present, every effort at housecleaning has failed after a few preliminary sweeps. Commerce dictates as strongly as ever. (p. 23)

Hans J. Lecky's survey in *T.V. News* indicates that Jones is correct. More than thirty per cent of all television time, Lecky calculates, is given to advertisement. Of the 1,000 hours in Lecky's sample, only 50 were "live." (((Lecky, pp. 93–94))) Moreover, the decline in "live" hours of commercial television may be directly proportional to the decline in quality. (((*Times*, p. 8)))

And so on, until your carded sources run out and your own resources take over completely.

YOUR FINAL DRAFT: DOCUMENTING YOUR SOURCES

Allow space for notes at the foot of the page. You can see from your preliminary drafts about how many footnotes will fall on your page, and about how much space to allow at the bottom. Allow plenty. You will begin your notes three spaces below your text. You have been double-spacing your text; now use a triple-space. Do *not* type a line between text and notes: this indicates a footnote continued from the preceding page. Single-space each note, but double-space between notes. Indent as for a paragraph. Type your number. Press the button at the end of your roller, and roll down about half the height of a capital letter. Begin typing your note without hitting the space bar: " ¹ Albert Kurtz, p. 5." After the first line, notes run out to the margin, as in paragraphs. The notes to our sample would come out like this:

> ¹ Donald Allenberg, *The Future of Television* (New York, 1968), p. 10; A. H. Hawkins, "Our Greatest Salesman," *American Thought*, IV (1971), 16; J. Weiss, "Government Control, a Growing Concern," *Saturday Night Journal*, September 20, 1968, p. 5; see especially W. W. Smith, "Television and the Modern World," *American Politician*, XIX (1965), 77: "This is creeping socialism. This is not the American way."
>
> ² "American Television and Responsibility," *Space*, August 16, 1964, pp. 23–25.
>
> ³ "Television and Vision: The Case for Governmental Control," *Independent Review*, VIII (1969), 20.
>
> ⁴ "A Survey of Programming," May 10, 1970, pp. 93–94.
>
> ⁵ "The Trouble with Television" (editorial), New York *Times*, April 10, 1968, Sec. 4, p. 8.

[Notice the comma here: omitted after "Television" and inserted after the parenthesis. Do the same with any parenthetical explanation of a title.]

Footnotes carry only information that does not appear in the text. In note 4, for example, only the title of the article, the date, and the pages appear, since the text gives the author and publication. Put as much in the text as possible, without cluttering it. You may have noticed that our long quotation from Jones carried "(p. 23)" at the end, without dropping down to a footnote, and that we needed no title, publication, or date because we had already given them. Use parentheses like this, even in your own sentences, once you have cited a source (notice where the periods and the quotation marks go):

> Jones further states that advertisers control hiring and firing (p. 24).
>
> Jones further states that "advertisers actually control hiring and firing, one way or another" (p. 24).

Punctuate your footnotes meticulously. The first three entries under our footnote 1 illustrate the three principal kinds of references:

BOOK

Donald Allenberg, *The Future of Television* (New York, 1968), p. 10.

QUARTERLY MAGAZINE

A. H. Hawkins, "Our Greatest Salesman," *American Thought,* IV (1971), 16. [Use volume number.]

POPULAR MAGAZINE

J. Weiss, "Government Control, a Growing Concern," *Saturday Night Journal,* September 20, 1968, p. 5. [Ignore volume number, if any.]

As in this last example, give the full date for a popular magazine, instead of Roman numerals and year, and *use no parentheses.* Newspaper articles (see our footnote 5, above) follow the same pattern. With a book, a popular magazine, or a newspaper you use "p." before the page number; with a magazine having a Roman volume number, do not use "p.": "XXIX (1919), 23–26." Give the second page number in full: "23–26" not "23–6." The point of footnoting, of course, is to identify author, title, publication, and page, to exhibit your sources fully to the reader, who might want to use them himself. Here are some complications:

> [1] Abraham B. Caldwell, "The Case for Subsidized Television," *American Questioner,* June 20, 1967, p. 37, quoted Albert N. Mendenhall, *The Time Is Now* (Princeton, 1969), p. 308.

[You have found the quotation in Mendenhall's book.]

> [1] D. C. Hill, "Who Is Communicating What?" in *Essays for Study,* ed. James L. McDonald and Leonard P. Doan (New York, 1969), p. 214, reprinted from *Era,* XII (1965).

[McDonald and Doan have edited the collection. You could have cited *Era* first, and given pages for both. A title ending in a question mark should not take a comma.]

[1] Arnold Peters, "Medicine," *Encyc. Brit.* (Chicago, 1964).

[Abbreviate familiar titles, so long as they remain clear. You need neither volume nor page numbers in alphabetized encyclopedias. Here the article was initialed "A.P.," and you have looked up the author's name in the Contributors' List.]

[1] "Prunes," *Encyc. Brit.* (Chicago, 1964).

[Here the article was not initialed.]

[1] George L. Gillies, "Robert Herrick's 'Corinna,' " *House and Home*, II (1881), 490.

[This shows where to put the comma when the title of a magazine article ends in a quotation, and you have to use both single and double quotation marks. Gillies's original title would have looked like this: Robert Herrick's "Corinna"]

[1] *The Merchant of Venice* I.ii.102, in *The Complete Works of Shakespeare*, ed. George Lyman Kittredge (Boston, 1936).

[Note the absence of the comma after the title, and the periods and close spacing between Act.scene.line. Subsequent references would go directly in your text within parentheses: (*Merch.* IV.iii.11–12). See further instructions below.]

These should cover most footnoting problems, or suggest how to meet them.

Abbreviate your references after the first full citation. Two old favorite abbreviations are now mercifully out of style. Do NOT use:

ibid.—*ibidem* ("in the same place"), meaning the title cited in the note directly before. Instead, use the author's last name, and give the page.

op. cit.—*opera citato* ("in the work cited"), meaning title referred to again after other notes have intervened. Again, use the author's last name instead, and give the page.

Four are still used and especially useful (do *not* italicize them):

cf.—*confer* (means "compare"); do not use it for "see."

et al.—*et alii* ("and others"); does not mean "and all"; use it after the first author in multiple authorships, "Ronald Elkins et al." —no comma.

loc. cit.—*loco citato* ("in the place cited"); use without page number, when you cite a page previously noted. Best in parentheses *in the text:* "Allenberg (loc. cit.) also considers this important."

passim—(not an abbreviation; a Latin word meaning "throughout the work; here and there"). Use when a writer makes the same point in many places within a single work; use also for statistics you have compiled from observations and tables scattered throughout his work.

Our footnotes to the television paper might continue like this, with abbreviations for works already fully cited:

> ⁶ Allenberg, p. 12.
> ⁷ Allenberg, p. 13.

[Would have been "Ibid., p. 13," but the name is clearer.]

> ⁸ Jones, passim.
> ⁹ Allenberg, p. 4.

[Would have been "Allenberg, op. cit., p. 4."]

> ¹⁰ Cf. Dillon et al., p. 191—exactly the opposite position.
> ¹¹ See Jones, p. 24, for a reasonable and full denial of this claim.
> ¹² See Weiss, p. 6, and Smith, p. 71.
> ¹³ Jones, loc. cit.; cf. Weiss, p. 3.

["Loc. cit." means the last Jones citation—p. 24—to which we are asking our readers to compare Weiss's position, indicating simply that Weiss is a little extreme.]

If we had two Joneses, our short references would simply have had to repeat first initials; if Jones had written two articles or books, we would have devised two convenient but clear short titles for subsequent references. In addition to Jones's article, "Television and Vision: The Case for Governmental Control," suppose we have also cited his book, *The Kinescopic Arts and Sciences* (Princeton, 1970). Our further references to him would look like this:

> ⁴ Jones, "Vision," p. 27.
> ⁵ Jones, *Kinescopic Arts*, p. 291.

Abbreviate books of the Bible, even the first time. The Bible and its books, though capitalized as ordinary titles, are never italicized. Biblical references go directly into your text, within parentheses—no footnote, no commas, *small* roman numerals for chapter, arabic for verse: Mark xvi.6; Jer. vi.24; II Sam. xviii.33. No comma—only a space—separates name from numbers; periods separate the numbers, *with no spacing.* The dictionary gives the accepted abbreviations: Gen., Exod., Lev., Deut. Make Biblical references like this:

> There is still nothing new under the sun (Eccl. i.9); man still does not live by bread alone (Matt. iv.4).
>
> As Ecclesiastes tells us, "there is no new thing under the sun" (i.9).

Abbreviate plays and long poems after the first time. Handle plays and long poems like Biblical citations, after an initial footnote that identifies the edition (see p. 132). Italicize the title: *Romeo* II.iv.72–75 [this is *Romeo and Juliet,* Act II, Scene iv, lines 72–75]; *Caesar* V.iii.6; *Ham.* I.i.23; *Iliad* IX.93; *P.L.* IV.918 [*Paradise Lost,* Book IV, line 918]. Use the numbers alone if you have already mentioned the title, or have clearly implied it, as in repeated quotations from the same work.

Match your bibliography to your footnotes. When your paper is finally typed, arrange the cards of the works cited in your footnotes in alphabetical order (by authors' last names or, with anonymous works, by first words of titles—ignoring initial *The, A,* or *An*). You will not have used all your notes, nor all the articles you have carded. In typing your bibliography, pass over them in decent silence. *Include no work not specifically cited.* Your bibliographical entries will be just like your footnotes except that: (1) you will put the author's last name first; (2) you will give the total span of pages for magazine articles—none at all for books; (3) you will reverse indentation so that the author's name will stand out; (4) you will punctuate differently—putting one period after the alphabetized name or title, and another (no parenthesis) after a *book's* place and date of publication; (5) you will include the publisher's name (New York: Thomas Y. Crowell Co., 1969) between the place and date; and (6) you will double-space, triple-spacing between entries. Your single-spacing has been the typewriter's approximation of passages set in small print. If you had been actually writing for print, you would have double-spaced everything and would not have put your footnotes at the bottoms of pages: you would have collected them serially at the end of the paper in a section headed "Footnotes." In many publications you would not have a bibliography; in many others, you would. Your research paper requires one, something like this:

BIBLIOGRAPHY

Allenberg, Donald. *The Future of Television.* New York: Nosuch Co., 1968.

Brown, J. P. "Some Facts about Television and Education," *New Mercury,* July 10, 1968, pp. 20–31.

Cummings, John L. "How Good Are Our Programs?" *Time and Tide,* XLVI (1962), 163–176.

Encyclopaedia Britannica. 14th ed. 24 vols. Chicago, 1952.

Jones, Bingham. *The Kinescopic Arts and Sciences.* Princeton: The Little House, Inc., 1970.

————. "Television and Vision: The Case for Governmental Control," *Independent Review,* VII (1969), 18–31.

"The Trouble with Television." Anon. editorial, New York *Times,* April 10, 1968, Sec. 4, p. 8.

[Each new section of this paper begins its numbering anew; hence, "Sec. 4." Notice that the city, which practically forms a part of the title, is nevertheless NOT italicized with newspapers: Kansas City *Star,* Detroit *Free Press.*]

I have based these instructions on *The MLA Style Sheet* (compiled by the Modern Language Association of America), which you may consult for further detail. It is standard for work in literature and the humanities. The sciences use slightly different conventions. Bingham Jones's article would look like this in a botanical bibliography (no italics, no quotation marks, no parentheses): Television and Vision: The Case for Governmental Control. Independent Review.8:18–31. For some advanced courses you may want to consult:

McCrum, Blanche, and Helen Jones. *Bibliographical Procedures & Style: A Manual for Bibliographers in the Library of Congress.* Washington, D.C.: Superintendent of Documents, 1954.

Publication Manual of the American Psychological Association. Washington, D.C., 1957.

13

old hat. [Wordy] Government television control should be
exercised by a committee of prominent citizens and
[awk] people interested in entertainment-type programs
appointed by the President. The people are interested
in T. V., and the people should be given a voice. [By] [?]
the use of A committee (T. V.) could be fairly and
effectively controlled. This would be Modern. [transition]

[DM] —Returning to finances, the companies could still place
their advertisements between shows, but they would not
control the shows. Advertising and showmanship would
be kept seperate. It would still sell soap and [ref.]
cigarettes and everything the public demands and maybe
make a contribution toward making this a better world — [trite]
in which to live, for not only the people but for the [// st]
advertisers too.

Sensible control would be both democratic and [// st]
help improve the intellectual level.

C — Idea good, plan good, research good — and your
argument is persuasive. You still can catch an
apt phrase now and then, BUT (!) you've fallen into
all your old habits in the rush. Avoid clusters of nouns
like government television control — 3 in a row! Avoid
the passive voice and all the excess wordage. The
end seems lame. And please learn to punctuate. This
deserves rewriting. Spend some time on it, sentence
by sentence. I'll be happy to reconsider the grade.

13

old hat." The government should control television only
through a committee of prominent citizens appointed by
the President. For balance, the committee should
include a few champions of light entertainment. Since,
in a sense, television is really public property, the
public should have some voice in television's affairs.
After all, representative government is the modern way.

Nor would business go unrepresented. Business
would still manage its own house, and it would have
seats on the governmental committee. Companies could
still bid for advertising space between the best programs,
but they could no longer influence the programs themselves.
Advertising would exercise its showmanship only in
advertising. It would still sell its soap and cigarettes,
but the programs themselves would be freed for variety
and creativity. New audiences might even benefit the
advertisers, and sensible control of the commercial
motive would certainly increase everyone's opportunity
to see for himself.

B+ Nice work! I like "champions of light entertainment"
and "see for himself." This is the style you've been
working for: not too big, not too little, sensible, clear,
on its toes. You are touching the concrete beautifully:
house, seats, soap and cigarettes.
Since this is a second chance, I can't give highest
honors. But it's a fine job. Congratulations. You're
really writing in Style ____ !

137

Style Manual. U.S. Government Printing Office. Rev. ed. Washington, D.C., 1959.

Style Manual for Biological Journals. Washington, D.C., 1960.

Turabian, Kate L. *A Manual for Writers of Term Papers, Theses, and Dissertations.* Rev. ed. Chicago: University of Chicago Press, 1955.

————. *Student's Guide for Writing College Papers.* Chicago: University of Chicago Press, 1963.

Wood, George McLane. *Suggestions to Authors . . . , United States Geological Survey.* 4th ed. rev. by Bernard H. Lane. Washington, D.C., 1935.

But for the present, let us suppose that you have finally turned your paper in. After all that researching, carding, plotting, revising, and typing, you are now dismayed as your instructor hands back your paper thoroughly penciled (with marks much like those inside the back cover of this book). Pages 136 and 137 give a sample of your trouble and of your final corrections. They should also demonstrate the value of a good antagonistic friend in helping you check our common tendency to become hypnotized by our own writing, and to stand convinced that our words say what we intended, when in fact they may say other things to our readers. If you have the foresight to plan and revise your writing against the Check List inside the front cover before submitting your paper in final form, you can save such a friend some trouble. You may even win his praise!

EXERCISES

1. Go to the card catalogue and pick a card, any card. Write down everything you can learn from it about the author and the book. Is it classified according to Dewey Decimal or the Library of Congress? What general category is it in—Philosophy, Agriculture? What can you surmise from the other numbers and letters of the call number? What other cards have probably been made for it? Record everything you can learn or guess from the single card. Now, find the book itself, and report everything else you can learn about it from the title page and the back of the title page.

2. Select some well-known literary work: *Walden, David Copperfield, Huckleberry Finn, Alice in Wonderland, The Wind in the Willows, A Farewell to Arms.* Describe how thoroughly it is catalogued by your

library. Check cards for author, title, and subject. How many editions does the library have? Is the work contained within any *Works?* How many cards treat it as a subject? Does your library own a first edition? This last may require that you find the date of the first edition by looking up your author in an encyclopedia, checking available books about him, and perhaps checking in the British Museum's *General Catalogue of Printed Books,* or, for a twentieth-century book, *United States Catalog of Printed Books* or *Cumulative Book Index* to discover the earliest cataloguing.

3. Read an article in one of the specialized encyclopedias, such as the *Catholic Encyclopedia,* the *Encyclopedia of World Art,* or the *Cyclopedia of American Government.* Then read articles on the same topic in two of the general encyclopedias, such as the *Britannica* and *Collier's.* Write an analysis that compares and evaluates the differing treatments.

4. Consult the current *World Almanac* for the date of some memorable event: the sinking of the *Titanic* or the *Lusitania,* Lindbergh's flight over the Atlantic, the United States' entry into war, the founding of the United Nations, the great stock-market crash, or the like. Now go to one of the other almanacs for the year of your event, and write an essay entitled, let us say, "1918"—a synopsis of the monumental and the curious for that year, as lively and interesting as you can make it.

5. Choose a subject—"Dog Racing," "Viet Nam," "Bowling," "Mushrooms," or what not—and write a short statistical report on the listings under this subject in the *Readers' Guide to Periodical Literature* over the past ten years. Does your subject have unusually fat or lean years? What kinds of magazines treat the subject? Can you infer anything from your data about fashions in magazines, or happenings in the world? Go to one article in the most prolific year to discover the reason for your subject's popularity.

6. Look up some event of the recent past (after 1913) in the *New York Times Index.* Write a paper on how the event is reported in the *Times* and in the other newspapers available in your library.

7. Write a brief description of four specialized indexes—for example, the *Art Index,* the *Dramatic Index,* the *Essay and General Literature Index,* the *Music Index*—telling what kinds of things you can learn from each, what kinds of things you would like to learn but cannot, and how convenient and informative each seems to be.

8. Selecting any well-known author, English or American (but to keep your task manageable, avoid such giants as Shakespeare and Milton), go to the "Annual Bibliography" in *PMLA* for any year, and copy out the year's crop of articles on your man. Now go to an appropriate specialized bibliography for the same year—the one in the *Philological Quarterly,* for instance, or in *Modern Philology* or in *American Literature* —and write a report comparing the differing treatments of the two.

SUGGESTED TOPICS FOR
RESEARCH PAPERS

Who Killed Malcolm X?
Socialized Medicine
Euthanasia
Capital Punishment
Early Reviews of *For Whom the Bell Tolls*
Lyndon B. Johnson's Foreign Policy
The Tonkin Gulf Incident
Light and Dark in Three Poems by Robert Frost

Interracial Marriage
Suffrage at Eighteen
Censorship
States' Rights
Federal Aid to Education
Chemotherapy for Psychosis
The Generation Gap
Assassination in Dallas
The Meaning of a Story by Faulkner
Legislation to Control Guns

Appendix:
A Glossary of Usage

Speech keeps daily pressure on writing, and writing returns the compliment, exacting sense from new twists in the spoken language and keeping old senses straight. Usage, generally, is "the way they say it." Usage provides the current, it keeps us afloat, it keeps us fresh—as it sweeps us along. But to distinguish himself the writer must always battle it, must always swim upstream. He may say, "Hooja-eatwith?"; but he will write: "With whom did they compare themselves? With the best, with whoever seemed admirable." Usage is, primarily, talk; and talk year by year gives words differing social approval, and differing meanings. Words move from the gutter to the penthouse, and back down the elevator shaft. *Bull,* a four-letter Anglo-Saxon word, was unmentionable in Victorian circles. One had to use *he-cow,* if at all. Phrases and syntactical patterns also have their fashions, mostly bad. *Like unto me* changes to *like me* to *like I do; this type of thing* becomes *this type thing; -wise,* after centuries of dormancy in only a few words (*likewise, clockwise, otherwise*), suddenly sprouts out the end of everything: *budgetwise, personalitywise, beautywise, prestigewise.* Suddenly, everyone is saying *hopefully.* As usual, the marketplace changes more than your money.

But the written language has always refined the language of the marketplace. The Attic Greek of Plato and Aristotle (as Aristotle's remarks about local usages show) was distilled from commercial exchange. Cicero and Catullus and Horace polished their currency against the archaic and the Greek. Mallarmé claimed that Poe had given *un sens plus pur aux mots de la tribu*—which Eliot rephrases for himself: "To purify the dialect of the tribe." It is the very nature of writing so to do; it is the writer's illusion that he has done so:

I have laboured to refine our language to grammatical purity, and to clear it from colloquial barbarisms, licentious idioms, and irregular combinations. Something, perhaps, I have added to the elegance of its construction, and something to the harmony of its cadence.

—wrote Samuel Johnson as he closed his *Rambler* papers. And he had almost done what he hoped. He was to shape English writing for the next hundred years, until it was ready for another dip in the stream and another purification. His work, moreover, lasts. We would not imitate it now; but we can read it with pleasure, and imitate its enduring drive for excellence.

Johnson goes on to say that he has "rarely admitted any word not authorized by former writers." Writers provide the second level of usage, the paper money. But even this usage requires principle. If we accept "what the best writers use," we still cannot tell whether it is sound: we may be aping their bad habits. John F. Kennedy's inaugural address, carefully polished by Harvard's best, contains this oddity (my italics): "For man holds in his mortal hands the power to abolish *all form* of human poverty and *all form* of human life." Clearly, he meant either *all forms* or *every form*—or *all* human poverty and *all* human life. This mixing of choices, this coupling of the collective *all* with singular *form*, can mean only something like "all traces of form," as if the President were melting a statue. Most singular indeed! Even the best go wrong.

So we cannot depend on usage for our rules. Usage is only a court of first appeal, where we can say no more than "He said it." Beyond that helpless litigation, we can test our writing by reason, and by simple principles: clarity is good, economy is good, ease is good, gracefulness is good, fullness is good, forcefulness is good. As with all predicaments on earth, we judge by appeal to principles, and we often find principles in conflict. Is it economical but unclear? Is it full but cumbersome? Is it clear but too colloquial for grace? Careful judgment will give the ruling.

Which is right, "I feel *bad*" or "I feel *badly*"? "The dress looks *good* on her" or "The dress looks *well* on her"? The man on the street would say, "I feel *bad*" and "The dress looks *good*," and he would be right: not because of "usage," but because *badly* would indicate shaky fingers and *well* a dress with good eyes. "Tie it tight" means "Tie it so that it is tight." Unfortunately, people trying to be proper follow the pattern of "He writes badly" and fall into the errors of "I feel badly" and "Tie it tightly." But *writes badly* is a verb with an adverb telling how the action is done, and *feel bad* is a verb with a predicate adjective modifying the subject and telling how the subject *is*. The predicate adjective describes existences, as in *ring true* and *come thick:* "they ring, and they are true"; "they come, and they are thick." So it is with other verbs pointing to states of being—*seem, appear, become, grow, sound, smell, taste*—on which "good usage" might rule the wrong way. Just remember that you don't say "I feel goodly." Let reason be your guide.

Likewise with *the reason . . . is because.* You can find this colloquial redundancy on many a distinguished page. But everything a good writer writes is not necessarily good. The phrase is a collision between two choices, as the mind rushes after its meaning: between (1) *the reason is that . . .* and (2) *it is . . . because.* Delete *the reason . . . is,* the colloquial pump-primer, and you save three words, sometimes four (the following eminent sentence, in which I have bracketed the surplus words, also suffers some redundancy of the *be's*):

> **In general it may be said that [the reason why] scholasticism was held to be an obstacle to truth [was] because it seemed to discourage further inquiry along experimental lines.**

And so, usage is perhaps where we begin; but if we end there, we may end in wordiness and mediocrity.

The following prescriptions are just about what the doctor ordered to keep you ticking, and in good company. They summarize the practices of the most careful writers—those who constantly attend to what words mean. They provide tips on avoiding wordiness, and avoiding those slips in diction that sometimes turn your reception a little chilly.

PRACTICAL PRESCRIPTIONS FOR GOOD WRITING

A, an. Use *a* before *h* sounded in an accented first syllable: *a HOSpital, a HAMburger.* Use *an* before a silent or an unaccented *h: an honor, an hisTORical event, an halLUcination.*

Above. For naturalness and effectiveness, avoid such references as "The above statistics are . . . ," and "The above speaks for itself." Simply use "These" or "This."

Aesthetic. An adjective: *an aesthetic judgment, his aesthetic viewpoint. Aesthetics* is singular for the science of beauty: "Santayana's *aesthetics* agrees with his metaphysics."

Affect. *Affect* means "to produce an *effect.*" Don't use it as a noun; just say *feeling* or *emotion. Affective* is jargon for *emotional* or *emotive.*

Aggravate. Means to add gravity to something already bad enough. Avoid using it to mean "irritate."

Wrong	*Right*
He aggravated his mother.	The rum aggravated his mother's fever.

All ready, already. Two different meanings. *All ready* means that everything is ready; *already* means "by this time."

All right, alright. *Alright* is not all right; you are confusing it with *already.*

Also. Do not use for *and:* not "*Also,* it failed," but simply "And it failed."

And/or. An ungainly hair-splitter and thought-stopper. You never *say* it. Don't write "for stage and/or screen"; write "for stage or screen, or both."

Anxious. Indicates *Angst,* agony, and anxiety. Does not mean cheerful expectation: "He was *anxious* to get started." Say *eager* instead.

Any. Don't link this singular adjective with plural ideas:

Poor	*Good*
He was the best of any senior in the class.	He was the best senior in the class.
If any people know the answer, they aren't talking.	If anyone knows the answer, he's not talking.

Anybody. Don't write it as two words—*any body*—unless you mean "any corpse," or other inanimate object (stellar body, body of water).

Any more. Always written as two words.

Anyone. Don't write it as two words—*any one*—unless you mean "any one thing."

Anyplace, someplace. Use *anywhere* and *somewhere* (adverbs), unless you mean "any *place*" and "some *place*."

Appearing. Don't write "an expensive appearing house." "An expensive-looking house" is not much better. Write "an expensive house," or "the house looked expensive."

Appreciate. Means "recognize the worth of." Do not use to mean simply "understand."

Loose	*Careful*
I appreciate your position.	I understand your position.
I appreciate that your position is grotesque.	I realize that your position is grotesque.

Around. Do not use for *about:* it will seem to mean "surrounding."

Poor	*Good*
Around thirty people came.	About thirty people came.
He sang at around ten o'clock.	He sang at about ten o'clock.

As. Use where the cigarette people have *like:* "It tastes good, *as* a goodie should." (See also *Like.*)

Do not use for *such as:* "Many things, *as* nails, hats, toothpicks . . . ." Write "Many things, *such as* nails . . . ."

Do not use for *because* or *since;* it is ambiguous:

Ambiguous	*Precise*
As I was walking, I had time to think.	*Since* I was walking, I had time to think.

Do not use *as* to mean "that" or "whether" (as in "I don't know *as* he would like her").

As . . . as. Use positively, not forgetting the second *as:*

Wrong	*Right*
as long if not longer than the other.	*as* long *as* the other, if not longer.

Negatively, use *not so . . . as:*

It is *not so* long *as the* other.
His argument is *not so* clear *as* it ought to be.
His argument is *neither so* clear *nor so* thorough *as* it ought to be.

As if. Takes the subjunctive:

as if he *were* cold

As of, as of now. Avoid, except for humor. Use *at,* or delete entirely.

Poor	*Improved*
He left as of ten o'clock.	He left at ten o'clock.
As of now, I've sworn off.	I've sworn off.
	I've just sworn off.

As to. Use only at the beginning of a sentence: "As to his first allegation, I can only say . . . ." Change it to *about,* or omit it, within a sentence: "He knows nothing *about* the details"; "He is not sure [as to] [whether] they are right."

At. Do not use after *where.* "Where is it *at?*" means "Where is it?"

Back of, in back of. *Behind* says it more smoothly.

Balance, bulk. Make them mean business, as in "He deposited the balance of his allowance" and "The bulk of the crop was ruined."

Do not use them for people.

Poor	*Improved*
The balance of the class went home.	The rest of the class went home.
The bulk of the crowd was indifferent.	Most of the crowd was indifferent.

Behalf—in your behalf, on your behalf. A nice distinction.

"He did it *in your behalf*" means he did it in your interest; "He did it *on your behalf*" means he was representing you, speaking for you.

Besides. Means "in addition to," not "other than."

Poor	Improved
Something besides smog was the cause. [unless smog was also a cause]	Something other than smog was the cause.

Better than. Unless you really mean *better than*, use *more than*.

Poor	Improved
The lake was better than two miles across.	The lake was more than two miles across.

Between, among. *Between* ("by twain") has *two* in mind; *among* has several. *Between*, a preposition, takes an object; *between us, between you and me*. ("Between you and I" is sheer embarrassment; see *me*, below.) But words sometimes fail us. "Between you and me and the gatepost" cannot conform to the rule and become "among you and me and the gatepost." *Between* seems to connote an intimate sharing *among* all concerned, each to each. *Between* seems also to indicate geographical placing: "It is midway between Chicago, Detroit, and Toledo." "The grenade fell between Jones and me and the gatepost"; but "The grenade fell among the fruit-stands." Keep *between* for two and *among* for three or more—unless sense forces a compromise. "Between every building was a plot of petunias" conveys the idea as nothing else will, however nonsensical "between a building" is.

Bimonthly, biweekly. Careless usage has damaged these almost beyond recognition, confusing them with *semimonthly* and *semiweekly*. For clarity, better say "every two months" and "every two weeks."

But, cannot but. "He can but fail" is old but usable. After a negative, however, the natural turn in *but* causes confusion:

Poor	Improved
He cannot *but* fail.	He can only fail.

He could not doubt but that
it . . . .

He could not doubt that
it . . . .

He could not help but
take . . . .

He could not help taking . . . .

Similarly, *but*'s too close or frequent keep your reader spinning:

Poor	*Improved*
The campaign was successful *but* costly. *But* the victory was sweet.	The campaign was costly, but victory was sweet.

When *but* means "except," it is a preposition.

Wrong	*Right*
Everybody laughed but I.	Everybody laughed but me.

But that, but what.   Colloquial redundancies.

Poor	*Improved*
No one doubts but that John's is the best steer.	No one doubts that John's is the best steer.
	John's is clearly the best steer.
There is no one but what would enjoy it.	Anyone would enjoy it.

Can, may (could, might).   Do not use *can* for permission, or possibility: "Can I see it?" means "Am I able to see it?" Use *may.* In assertions, the distinction is clear: "He can do it." "He may do it." "If he can, he may."

Could and *might* are the past tenses, but when used in the present time they are subjunctive, with shades of possibility, and hence politeness: "*Could* you come next Tuesday?" "*Might* I inquire about your plans?" *Could* may mean ability almost as strongly as *can:* "I'm sure he could do it." But *could* and *might* are usually subjunctives, expressing doubt:

Perhaps he could make it, if he tried.
I might be able to go, but I doubt it.

Can't hardly, couldn't hardly.   Use *can hardly, could hardly.*

Case.   Chop out this deadwood:

Poor	*Improved*
In many cases, ants survive	Ants often . . . .
In such a case, surgery is recommended.	Then surgery is recommended.
In case he goes	If he goes . . . .
Everyone enjoyed himself, except in a few scattered cases.	Almost everyone enjoyed himself.

Cause-and-effect relationship.   Verbal adhesive tape. Recast the sentence, with some verb other than the wordy *cause:*

Poor	*Improved*
Othello's jealousy rises in a cause-and-effect relationship when he sees the handkerchief.	Seeing the handkerchief arouses Othello's jealousy.

Center around.   A physical impossibility. *Centers on,* or *revolves around,* or *concerns,* or *is about.*

Circumstances.   *In these circumstances* makes more sense than *under these circumstances,* since the stances are standing around (*circum*), not standing under.

Clichés.   Don't use unwittingly. But they can be effective. There are two kinds: (1) the literary—*tried and true, the not too distant future, sadder but wiser, in the style to which she had become accustomed;* (2) the proverbial—*apple of his eye, skin of your teeth, sharp as a tack, quick as a flash, twinkling of an eye.* The literary ones are rhetorical, clinched by sound alone; the proverbial are metaphors caught in the popular fancy.

The proverbial cliché can lighten a dull passage. You may even revitalize them (see p. 93). Avoid the literary, unless you turn them to your advantage: *tried and untrue, gladder and wiser, a future not too distant.*

Compare to, compare with.   To compare *to* is to show similarities (and differences) between different kinds; to compare *with* is to show differences (and similarities) between like kinds.

Composition has been compared *to* architecture.

He compares favorably *with* Mickey Spillane.
Compare Shakespeare *with* Ben Jonson.

Comparisons.   Make them complete; add a *than:*

It is more like a jigsaw puzzle *than a rational plan.*
They are more thoughtful *than the others.*
The first is better *than the second.* (Or "The first is *the* better.")

Connected with, in connection with.   Always wordy. Say *about, with,* or *in.*

Poor	Improved
They discussed several things connected with history.	They discussed several historical questions.
They liked everything in connection with the university.	They liked everything about the university.
He is connected with the Smith Corporation.	He is with the Smith Corporation.

Consider, consider as.   The first means "believe to be"; the second, "think about" or "speak about": "I consider him excellent." "I consider him first as a student, then as a man."

Contact.   Don't *contact* anyone: get in touch with him, call him, write him, find him, tell him. Don't make a good *contact,* make a helpful friend.

Continual, continuous.   You can improve your writing by *continual* practice, but the effort cannot be *continuous.* The first means "frequently repeated"; the second, "without interruption."

It requires continual practice.
He saw a continuous line of clouds.

Couple.   Use *two, a few,* or *several.* Only the breeziest occasions will allow *a couple of.*

Curriculum.   The plural is *curricula;* the adjective, *curricular.*

The school offers three separate curricula.
Extracurricular activities also count.

Data.   A plural, like *curricula, strata, phenomena:*

The data are inconclusive.

Definitely.   A high-school favorite. Cut it out.

Different than.   Never use it. Things differ *from* each other. Only in comparing differences could *than* be used: "All three of his copies differ from the original, but his last one is *more* different *than* the others." But here *than* is controlled by *more*, not by *different*.

Wrong	*Right*
It is different *than* I expected.	It is different *from* what I expected.
	It is not what I expected.
This is different *than* all the others.	This is different *from* all the others.

Disinterested.   Does not mean "uninterested." *Disinterested* means impartial, without private interests in the issue.

Wrong	*Right*
You seem disinterested in the case.	You seem uninterested in the case.
	The judge was disinterested and perfectly fair.

Due to.   Never begin a sentence with "*Due to* circumstances beyond his control, he . . . ." *Due* is an adjective and must always relate to a noun or pronoun: "The catastrophe *due to* circumstances beyond his control was unavoidable," or "The catastrophe was *due to* circumstances beyond his control" (predicate adjective). But you are still better off with *because of, through, by,* or *owing to. Due to* is usually a symptom of wordiness, especially when it leads to *due to the fact that.*

Wrong	*Right*
He resigned due to sickness.	He resigned because of sickness.
He succeeded due to hard work.	He succeeded through hard work.
He lost his shirt due to leaving it in the locker room.	He lost his shirt by leaving it in the locker room.

The Far East will continue to worry the West, due to a general social upheaval.	The Far East will continue to worry the West, owing to a general social upheaval.

Due to the fact that. A venerable piece of plumbing meaning *because*.

Jargon	*Improved*
The program failed due to the fact that a recession had set in.	The program failed because a recession had set in.

Effect. As a noun, it means "result"; as a verb, "to bring about" (not to be confused with *to affect*, meaning "to concern, impress, touch, move"—or "pretend").

What was the effect?
He effected a thorough change.
How did it affect you?

Enormity. Means "atrociousness"; does not mean "enormousness."

the enormity of the crime
the enormousness of the mountain

Enthuse. Don't use it; it coos and gushes:

Wrong	*Right*
She *enthused* over her new dress.	She gushed on and on about her new dress.
He was *enthused*.	He was enthusiastic.

Equally as good. A redundant mixture of two choices, *as good as* and *equally good*. Use only one at a time.

Etc. Substitute something specific for it, or drop it, or use something like *and so forth:*

Poor	*Improved*
She served fruit, cheese, candies, etc.	She served fruit, cheese, candies, and little sweet pickles.
	She served fruit, cheese, candies, and the like.

Ethic.   A mannered rendition of *ethics,* the singular and plural noun meaning a system or science of moral principles. Even poorer as an adjective for *ethical.*

Exists.   Another symptom of wordiness.

Poor	Improved
a system like that which exists at the university	a system like that at the university

the fact that.   Deadly with *due to,* often sickening by itself.

Poor	Improved
The fact that Rome fell due to moral decay is clear.	That Rome fell through moral decay is clear.
This disparity is in part a result of the fact that some of the best indicators make their best showings in an expanding market.	This disparity arises in part because some of the best indicators . . . .

Factor.   Avoid it. We've used it to death. Try *element,* when you mean "element." Look for an accurate verb when you mean "cause."

Poor	Improved
The increase in female employment is a factor in juvenile delinquency.	The increase in female employment has contributed to juvenile delinquency.
Puritan self-sufficiency was an important factor in the rise of capitalism.	Puritan self-sufficiency favored the rise of capitalism.

Farther, further.   The first means distance; the second, time or figurative distance. You look *farther* and consider *further.*

The field of.   Try to omit it—you usually can—or bring the metaphor to life.

Poor	Improved
He is studying in the field of geology.	He is studying geology.

| He changed from the field of science to fine arts. | He moved from the field of science to the greener pasture of fine arts. |

Firstly. Archaic. Trim all such terms to *first, second, third,* and so on.

Fix. The word means "to establish in place"; it means "to repair" only in speech or colloquial writing.

Flaunt, flout. *Flaunt* means to parade, to wave impudently; *flout* means to scoff at. The first is metaphorical; the second, not: "She *flaunted* her wickedness and *flouted* the police."

Folks. Write *parents, mother and father,* or *family* instead.

Former, latter. Passable, but they make the reader look back. Repeating the antecedents is better.

Poor	*Improved*
The Athenians and Spartans were always in conflict. *The former* had a better civilization; *the latter* had a better army.	The Athenians and Spartans were always in conflict. Athens had the better culture; Sparta, the better army.

Gray. America prefers *gray;* England, *grey*—matching our initials.

Hanged, hung. *Hanged* is the past of *hang* only for the death penalty.

They hung the rope and hanged the man.
The rope was hung; the man was hanged.

Hardly. Watch the negative here. "I can't *hardly*" means "I *can* easily." Write: "One can hardly conceive the vastness."

Hopefully. An inaccurate dangler, a popular cliché. "Hopefully, they are at work" does not mean that they are working hopefully. Simply use "I hope." Not "They are a symbol of idealism, and, hopefully, are representative," but "They symbolize idealism, and are, I hope, representative."

However.   Bury it between commas, or replace it with *but* or *nevertheless.*

Poor	Improved
However, the day had not been entirely lost.	*But* the day had not been entirely lost.
However, the script that Alcuin invented became the forerunner of modern handwriting.	The script that Alcuin invented, *however,* became the forerunner of modern handwriting.

Initial *however* should be an adverb:

However long it takes, it will be done.
However she did it, she did it well.

The idea that.   Like *the fact that*—and the cure is the same.

Poor	Improved
He liked the idea that she was going.	He was pleased she was going.
The idea that space is infinite is difficult to grasp.	That space is infinite is difficult to grasp.

Identify.   Give it an object:

He *identified the wallet.*
He *identified himself* with the hero. (*Not* "He identified with the hero.")

Image.   Resist its popularity, make it mean what it says, and never make it a verb. Do NOT say, "The university should *image* the handsome intellectual."

Imply, infer.   The author *implies;* you *infer* ("carry in") what you think he means.

He *implied* that all women were hypocrites.
From the ending, we *infer* that tragedy ennobles as it kills.

Importantly.   Often an inaccurate (and popular) adverb, like *hopefully.*

Inaccurate	Improved
More importantly, he walked home.	More important, he walked home.

He did not walk home importantly, nor more importantly.

Inside of, outside of. "They painted the *outside of* the house" is sound usage; but these expressions can be redundant and inaccurate.

Poor	Improved
inside of half an hour	within half an hour
He had nothing for dinner outside of a few potato chips.	He had nothing for dinner but a few potato chips.

Instances. Redundant. *In many instances* means *often, frequently.*

Interesting. Make what you say interesting, but never tell the reader *it is interesting:* he may not believe you. *It is interesting* is merely a lazy preamble:

Poor	Improved
It is interesting to note that nicotine is named for Jean Nicot, who introduced tobacco into France in 1560.	Nicotine is named for Jean Nicot, who introduced tobacco into France in 1560.

Irony. Not the same as sarcasm (which see). A clash between appearance and reality. Irony may be either comic or tragic, depending on your view. But, comic or tragic, irony is of three essential kinds:

Verbal irony. You say the opposite of what you mean: "It's a *great* day," appearing to mean *great* but really meaning *terrible.*

Dramatic irony. Someone unwittingly states a contrary to the truth. A character in a play, for example, might say "This is my great day," after the audience has just seen his daughter abducted and the mortgage foreclosed.

Irony of circumstance. The opposite of what ought to happen happens (it rains on the day of the Weather Bureau's picnic; the best man of all is killed); and we are sharply aware of the contrast.

Irregardless. No such word. The *ir-* (meaning "not") is doing what the *-less* already does. You are thinking of *irrespective,* and trying to say *regardless.*

-ize. A handy way to make verbs from nouns and adjectives (*patron-ize, civil-ize*). But handle with care. Manufacture new *-izes* only with a sense of humor and daring ("they Harvardized the party"). Business overdoes the trick: *finalize,* a relative newcomer, has provoked strong disapproval from writers not commercially familiarized.

Kind of, sort of. Colloquialisms for *somewhat, rather, something,* and the like. "It *is kind of* odd" will not get by. But "It is a *kind of* academic hippopotamus" will get by nicely, because *a kind of* means *a species of.* Change "a kind of a poor sport" to "a kind of poor sport," and you will seem as knowledgeable as a scientist.

Lay. Don't use *lay* to mean *lie. Lay* means "to put" and needs an object; *lie* means "to recline." Memorize both their present and past tenses, which are frequently confused:

I *lie* down when I can; I *lay* down yesterday; I have *lain* down often. [Intransitive, no object.]

The hen *lays* an egg; she *laid* one yesterday; she has *laid* four this week. [Transitive, *lays* an object.]

Now I *lay* the book on the table; I *laid* it there yesterday; I have *laid* it there many times.

Lend, loan. Don't use *loan* for *lend. Lend* is the verb; *loan,* the noun: "Please *lend* me a five; I need a *loan* badly." Remember the line from the song: "I'll *send* you to a *friend* who'll be willing to *lend.*"

Less, few. Do not use one for the other. *Less* answers "How much?" *Few* answers "How many?"

Wrong	*Right*
We had *less* people than last time.	We had *fewer* people this time than last.

Like, as, as if. Learn to distinguish these three. *Like* is a preposition, taking an object; when a verb follows, use *as* or *as if:*

He looks *like* me.
He dresses *as* I do.
He acts *as if* he *were* mad.

Note that *like* takes the objective case, and that *as,* being a conjunction, is followed by the nominative:

She looks like *her*.
He is as tall as *I* [am].
He is tall, like *me*.

The pattern of the prepositional phrase (*like me, like a house, like a river*) has caused *like* to replace *as* where no verb follows in phrases other than comparisons (*as . . . as*):

It works *like* a charm. (*. . . as* a charm *works.*)
It went over *like* a lead balloon. (*. . . as* a lead balloon *does.*)
They worked *like* beavers. (*. . . as* beavers *do.*)

Notice that *as* would give these three statements a meaning of substitution or disguise: "It works as a charm" (but it really isn't a charm); "It went over as a lead balloon" (disguised as a lead balloon).

Manner. Drop this from your working vocabulary. *In a . . . manner* is a favorite redundancy. Replace it with an adverb: *in a clever manner* means "cleverly"; *in an awkward manner* means "awkwardly."

Me. Use *me* boldly. It is the proper object of verbs and prepositions. Nothing is sadder than faulty propriety: "between you and *I*," or "They gave it to John and *I*," or "They invited my wife and *I*." Test yourself by dropping the first member: "between I" (*no*), "gave it to I" (*no*), "invited I" (*no*). And do not substitute *myself*.

Medium, media. The singular and the plural. Avoid *medias*, and you will distinguish yourself from the masses.

Most. Does not mean "almost."

Wrong	*Right*
Most everyone knows.	Almost everyone knows.

Myself. Use it only reflexively ("I hurt *myself*"), or intensively ("I *myself* often have trouble"). Fear of *me* leads to the incorrect "They gave it to John and *myself*." Do not use *myself, himself, herself, themselves* for *me, him, her, them.*

Nature. Avoid this padding. Do not write *moderate in nature, moderate by nature, of a moderate nature;* simply write *moderate.*

Near. Avoid using it for degree:

Poor	*Improved*
a near perfect orbit	a nearly perfect orbit
	an almost perfect orbit
We are nowhere near knowledgeable enough.	We are not nearly knowledgeable enough.
It was a near disaster.	It was nearly a disaster [or "nearly disastrous"].

None. This pronoun means "no one" and takes a singular verb, as do *each, every, everyone, nobody,* and other distributives. *None are* has been common and admissible for centuries, but *none is* holds its own, with a certain prestige, even in the daily newspaper. Another pronoun referring back to any of these must also be singular.

Poor	*Improved*
None of them *are* perfect.	None of them *is* perfect.
Every one of the men *eat* a big breakfast.	Every one of the men *eats* a big breakfast.
Everybody thinks *they have* the worst of it.	Everybody thinks *he has* the worst of it.

No one. Always two words, not *noone,* nor *no-one.*

Off of. Write *from:* "He jumped *from* his horse."

One. Avoid this common redundancy.

Poor	*Improved*
One of the most effective ways of writing is rewriting.	The best writing is rewriting.
The Ambassadors is one of the most interesting of James's books.	*The Ambassadors* is James at his best.
The meeting was obviously a poor one.	The meeting was obviously poor.

In constructions such as "one of the best that . . ." and "one of the worst who . . . ," the relative pronouns often are mistakenly considered singular. The plural noun of the prepositional phrase (*the best, worst*), not *the one*, is the antecedent, and the verb must be plural too:

Wrong	*Right*
one of the best (*players*) who *has* ever swung a bat	one of the best (*players*) who *have* ever swung a bat

Only. Don't put it in too soon; you will say what you do not mean.

Wrong	*Right*
He *only liked* mystery stories.	He liked *only mystery* stories.

Participle for gerund. Avoid this frequent confusion of the *-ings*. The participle works as an adjective; the gerund, as a noun. You want gerunds in the following constructions, and you can get them by changing the misleading noun or pronoun to the possessive case:

Wrong	*Right*
Washington commended *him passing* through the British lines.	Washington commended *his passing* through the British lines.
Do you mind *me staying* late?	Do you mind *my staying* late?
She disliked *Bill smoking*.	She disliked *Bill's smoking*.
We all enjoyed *them singing* songs and *having* a good time.	We all enjoyed *their singing* songs and *having* a good time.

You can catch these errors by asking yourself if you mean that "Washington commended *him*," or that "She disliked *Bill*" (which you do not).

Per. Use *a:* "He worked ten hours *a* day." *Per* is jargonish.

Perfect. Not "more perfect," but "more nearly perfect."

Personal. Change "personal friend" to "good friend," and protect him from seeming too personal.

Personally. Always superfluous.

Poor	Improved
I want to welcome them *personally*.	I want to welcome them [myself].
Personally, I like it.	I like it.

Phase. *Phase* is not *faze* ("daunt"), nor does it mean "aspect" or "part"; it is a stage in a familiar cycle, like that of the moon or the caterpillar.

Picket. A pointed fence-post, or a person so staked. *To picket* is to deploy people as pickets, or to join with others as a protesting fence against wrongs.

Poor	Improved
They began a picket of	They began to picket . . . .
They began their picket	They began picketing . . . .
Until they withdraw their picket	Until they withdraw their pickets . . . .

Plan on. Use *plan to*.

Wrong	Right
He planned on going.	He planned to go.

Power vacuum. A physical contradiction. Delete the *power*, or put it where it belongs, and your phrase will be accurate.

Prejudice. The illiterate are beginning to write "He was *prejudice*." Their readers are outrage.

Proof, evidence. *Proof* results from enough *evidence* to establish a point beyond doubt. Be modest about claiming proof:

Poor	Improved
This *proves* that Fielding was in Bath at the time.	Evidently, Fielding was in Bath at the time.

Proved, proven. *Proved* is the past participle, which may serve as an adjective meaning "successfully tested or demonstrated"; *proven* is an adjective only, and means "tested by time":

Wrong	Right
It has proven true. [past part.]	It has proved true.
a proven theory [past part. as adj.]	a proved theory
The theory was proven. [same]	The theory was proved.
a proved remedy [pure adj.]	a proven remedy

Quality. Keep it as a noun. Too many *professional quality writers* are cluttering our prose, and *poor in quality* means "poor."

Quote, quotation. Quote your quotations, and put them in quotation marks. Distinguish the verb from the noun. The best solution is to use *quote* as a verb and to find synonyms for the noun: *passage, remark, assertion.*

Real. Do not use for *very*. *Real* is an adjective meaning "actual":

Wrong	Right
It was *real* good.	It was *very* good.
	It was *really* good.

Reason . . . is because. Knock out *the reason . . . is*, and you will have a good sentence.

[The reason] they have difficulty with languages [is] because they have no interest in them.

Regarding, in regard to. Redundant or inaccurate.

Poor	Improved
Regarding the banknote, Jones was perplexed. [Was he *looking* at it?]	Jones was perplexed by the banknote.
He knew nothing *regarding* money.	He knew nothing about money.
She was careful *in regard to* the facts.	She respected the facts.

Respective, respectively. Redundant.

Poor	Improved
The armies retreated to their *respective* trenches.	The armies retreated to their trenches.

| Smith and Jones won the first and second prize *respectively*. | Smith won the first prize; Jones, the second. |

Round. British for *around*.

Sanction. Beatifically ambiguous, now meaning both "to approve" and "to penalize." But why contribute to confusion? Stick to the root; use it only "to bless," "to sanctify," "to approve," "to permit." Use *penalize* or *prohibit* when you mean just that.

| *Poor* | *Improved* |
| They exacted sanctions. | They exacted penalties. |

Sarcasm. The student's word for irony. Sarcasm intends personal hurt. It may also be ironic, but need not be. "Well, little man, what now?" is pure sarcasm when a dwarf interrupts the class; it is ironic sarcasm when a seven-footer bursts in. See *Irony*.

Shall, will; should, would. Keep *shall* and *should* for *I* and *we*, and *will* and *would* for the others. Switch them to express determination: "*I will* go; *they shall* not pass."

Similar to. Use *like:*

| *Poor* | *Improved* |
| This is *similar to* that. | This is *like* that. |

Slow. GO SLOW is what the street signs and the men on the street all say, but write "go slowly."

So. Should be followed by *that* in describing extent: "It was *so* foggy *that* traffic almost stopped." Avoid its incomplete form, the schoolgirl's intensive—*so nice, so wonderful, so pretty*—though occasionally this is effective.

Split infinitives. Improve them. They are cliché traps: *to really know, to really like, to better understand.* They are misleaders: *to better . . . , to further . . . , to well . . . , to even . . . . To better know* is to make *know* better; *to even like* is to make *like* even, all of which is nonsense. Indeed, in perverse moments *to eventually go* seems to say that *go* is being "eventualied." Finally, they are usually redundant: *to really understand* is *to understand.* The quickest cure for split infinitives is to drop the adverb.

Even the splitters do not recommend splitting as a rule. The rule remains DON'T SPLIT; and if you must, learn what you are doing —a little deviltry is better for the soul than ignorance. But I am convinced that you can always mend the split for a gain in grace, and often for a saving of words. You can sometimes change the adverb to an adjective: "to adequately think out solutions" can become "to think out adequate solutions." Or you can drop the adverb —often exuberant—or bring it forward, or move it along:

Poor	*Improved*
I cannot bring myself to really like the fellow.	I cannot bring myself to like the fellow.
	I cannot bring myself really to like the fellow.
	I really cannot bring myself to like the fellow.

George O. Curme gives the following examples from eminent splitters, arguing that usage makes them right.* But each of them can be improved:

Poor	*Improved*
I wish the reader to clearly understand this. (Ruskin)	I wish the reader to understand this.
	I wish the reader to understand this clearly.
It would have overburdened the text to there incorporate many details. (Hempl, *Mod. Lang. Notes*)	Details would have overburdened the text.
. . . without permitting himself to actually mention the name. (Arnold)	. . . without permitting himself to mention the name.
. . . of a kind to directly stimulate curiosity. (Pater)	. . . of a kind to stimulate curiosity.
	. . . of a kind to stimulate curiosity directly.
. . . things which few except parents can be expected to really understand. (Oliver Wendell Holmes)	. . . things only parents can understand.

* *English Grammar* (New York: Barnes and Noble, 1947).

. . . to   bravely   disbelieve   . . . bravely to disbelieve
(Browning, *The Ring and
the Book,* Cambridge ed., p.
570)

Browning's line, in fact, would have thumped somewhat less if he
had dared bravely to vary his meter and mend his infinitive like
this:

Whence need bravely to disbelieve report

Structure. A darling of the jargoneer, often meaning nothing
more framelike than "unity" or "coherence." *Plot structure* usually
means "plot," with little idea of beams and girders. Use it only for
something you could diagram, like the ribs of a snake, and never
use it as a verb.

Poor	*Improved*
He structured the meeting.	He organized (planned, arranged) the meeting.

That, which, who. *That* defines and restricts; *which* is explanatory and nonrestrictive; *who* stands for people, and may be restrictive or nonrestrictive. (See pp. 52; 79–80.)

The faucet *that* drips is in the basement.
The faucet, *which* drips badly, needs attention.
Of all the Democrats *who* supported him at first, none was more
   ardent than Jones.
Of all the Democrats, *who* supported him at first, none was more
   ardent than Jones.

There is, there are, it is. *C'est dangereusement verbeux.* In
French, it is almost as necessary as breathing. In English, it is
natural, convenient—and wordy. Notice that *it* has here been referring to something specific, differing distinctly from the *it* in "It
is easy to write badly." This indefinite subject, as also with *there is*
and *there are,* gives the trouble. Of course, you will occasionally
need an *it* or a *there* to assert existences:

There are ants in the cupboard.
There is only one Kenneth.
There are craters on the moon.
It is too bad.

But avoid *there is* and *it is,* and you will avoid some sludgy traps. They are part of the spoken language, like clearing the throat, and they frequently add just as little, especially when entailing a *that* or a *which:*

> There are three men on duty. [Three men are on duty.]
> It is a shame that they had no lawyer. [Unfortunately, they had no lawyer.]
> There are two things which are important here. [Two things are important here.]
> There is nothing wrong with this. [Nothing is wrong with this.]
> It is a habit which few can break. [Few can break this habit.]

They.   A loose indefinite pronoun; tighten it:

Poor	*Improved*
They are all against us, you know.	*Everyone* is against us, you know.
They launch our rockets at Cape Kennedy.	The *United States* launches its rockets from Cape Kennedy.

Do not use *they* with a singular antecedent.

Wrong	*Right*
Everyone knows *they* should write correctly.	*Everyone* knows *he* should write correctly.
Every one of the students assumes *they* will pass.	*Every one* of the students assumes *he* will pass.

Till, until.   Both are respectable. Note the spelling. Do not write *'til.*

Too.   Awful as a conjunctive adverb: "Too, it was unjust." Also poor as an intensive: "They did not do too well" (note the difference in Shakespeare's "not wisely but too well"—he really means it). Write *very,* or (better) nothing: "They did not do well."

Trite.   From Latin *tritus:* "worn out." Many words get temporarily worn out and unusable: *emasculated, viable, situation,* to name a few. And many phrases are permanently frayed; see *Clichés.*

Try and.   Write *try to. To try and do* means *to try and to do,* which is probably not what you mean.

Type. Banish it, abolish it. If you must use it, insert *of:* not *that type person* but *that type OF person,* though even this is really jargon for *that kind of person, a person like that.* The newspapers have succumbed, and we hear of *commando-type forces* for *commando forces,* of *a Castro-type dictator* for *another Castro.* The most accurate translations of *-type* are *-like, -ish, -esque,* and *-ate,* depending on sense and euphony: *Castro-like, Castro-ish, Russianesque, Italianate.* English has many ways of saying it:

Wrong	*Right*
Mondrian's checkerboard-type painting	Mondrian's checkerboard of a painting
	Mondrian's checkerboardish painting
	Mondrian's checkerboard-like painting
French-type dressing	French dressing
Italian-type spaghetti	Italian spaghetti [Be bold!—we neither know nor care whether it's imported.]
atomic-type submarine	atomic submarine
She was a Brigitte Bardot-type girl.	She was like Brigitte Bardot.
	She was a Brigitte Bardot.
	She was a Brigitte Bardot kind of girl.
	She was a Brigitte Bardot type.
an apprentice-type situation	apprenticeship
a string-type playpen	a string playpen
a Puck-type person	a Puckish person, a Puck-like person

Unique. Something *unique* has nothing else in the world like it.

Wrong	*Right*
The more unique the plan	The more nearly unique . . . .
the most unique man I know	the most unusual man I know
a very unique personality	a unique personality

Use, use of. A dangerously wordy word. "Through [the use of] personification, he asserts a theme." "In this sense, [the use of] physical detail is significant."

Poor	*Improved*
He uses personification	He personifies . . . .
He uses inductive reasoning	He reasons inductively . . . .

Utilize, utilization. Wordy. *Utilize* means "use" (verb). *Utilization* means "the use" (noun). And the whole idea of *using*—a basic concept—is frequently contained in the other words of your sentence.

Poor	*Improved*
He *utilizes* frequent dialogue to enliven his stories.	Frequent dialogue enlivens his stories
The utilization of a scapegoat eases their guilt.	A scapegoat eases their guilt.

Very. Spare the *very* and the *quite, rather, pretty,* and *little.* I would hate to admit (and don't care to know) how many of these qualifiers I have cut from this text. You can do without them entirely.

Ways. Means *way:* "He went a short *way* into the woods."

While. Reserve for time only, as in "*While* I was talking, she smoked constantly."

Wrong	*Right*
While I like her, I don't admire her.	*Although* I like her, I don't admire her.
The side roads were impassable, *while* the highways were clear.	The side roads were impassable, *but* the highways were clear.
The seniors eat in clubs, *while* the freshmen eat in their dormitories.	The seniors eat in clubs, *and* the freshmen eat in their dormitories.

Whom. The objective form, after verbs and prepositions; but it is often wrongly put as the subject of a clause.

Wrong	Right
Give the ticket to *whomever* wants it.	Give the ticket to *whoever* wants it. [The whole clause is the object of *to; whoever* is the subject of *wants.*]
The president, *whom* he said would be late	The president, *who* he said would be late . . . . [Commas around *he said* would clear the confusion.]
Whom shall I say called?	Who shall I say called?

BUT:

They did not know whom to elect. [The infinitive takes the objective case.]

-wise. Avoid all confections like *marketwise, customerwise, pricewise, gradewise, confectionwise.*

Would. For habitual acts, the simple past is more economical:

Poor	Improved
The parliament *would meet* only when called by the king.	The parliament *met* only when called by the king.
Every hour, the watchman *would make* his round.	Every hour, the watchman *made* his round.

Would sometimes seeps into the premise of a supposition. Rule: Don't use *would* in an *if*-clause.

Wrong	Right
If he *would have* gone, he would have succeeded.	If he *had gone,* he would have succeeded.
	Had he gone, he would have succeeded [more economical].
I wish I *would have* learned it.	I wish I *had* learned it.

Index

Index

verbs *(cont.)*
  tense of, methods of establishing, 65–66
  see also gerunds; infinitives; participles; split infinitives
very, 168
vocabulary, 87–94
  abstract and concrete words in, 90
  for clarity, 94–95
  for distinction, 95
  and finding the right word, 97
  and metaphor, 91–94
  methods of increasing, 87–89
  range, 95–96
  and word origins, 87, 88–89, 95–96, 100–101
  and word substitutions, 88
  see also spelling; usage; specific words
vowels, pronunciation of, as spelling aid, 100

was, monotony and, 50
way, manner, 88
ways, 168
well, good, 142–143
when, as subordinator, 31, 32
which
  overuse of, 50, 51–52
  as relative pronoun, 52, 165
  see also of-and-*which* disease
which are, avoiding, 52
while, 168
White, E. B.
  on ablative absolute, 36
  quoted, 32, 75

Whitehead, Alfred North, quoted, 52
who
  overuse of, 50, 51, 52
  as relative pronoun, 52, 165
  singular vs. plural verb with, 62
who are, avoiding, 52
whom, 50, 51, 168–169
will, shall, 163
Woolf, Virginia, quoted, 42–43, 77
wordiness, avoiding, 47–48, 49, 50–51, 53, 96–99
words (*see* diction; vocabulary)
World Almanac and Book of Facts, The, 124
would, 169
would, should, 163
writing the essay
  argumentative stand in, 2–7, 11–14
  beginning paragraphs in, 10–12, 18–20, 25, 107
  end paragraphs in, 9–10, 22–24, 25, 108
  and increasing reader's interest, 10–11
  keyhole plan of whole, 24, 25
  middle paragraphs in, 9, 10–14, 20–22, 25, 107–108
  point arrangement in, 10–11
  see also autobiographical essay; ironic essay; paragraphs; research papers; sentences; terrible essay; thesis

yet
  comma with, 74, 76
  use of, 60